JESUS CHRIST

Available in The Heart of Christian Faith Series

Faith and Creeds: A Guide for Study and Devotion
The Living God: A Guide for Study and Devotion

JESUS CHRIST

A Guide for Study and Devotion

Alister E. McGrath

WESTMINSTER
JOHN KNOX PRESS
LOUISVILLE · KENTUCKY

© 2014 Alister E. McGrath

First published in the United States of America in 2014 by
Westminster John Knox Press
100 Witherspoon Street
Louisville, KY 40202

First published in Great Britain in 2014 by
Society for Promoting Christian Knowledge
36 Causton Street
London SW1P 4ST

14 15 16 17 18 19 20 21 22 23—10 9 8 7 6 5 4 3 2 1

Cover design by designpointinc.com
Typeset by Graphicraft Limited, Hong Kong

Library of Congress Cataloging-in-Publication Data
McGrath, Alister E., 1953-
Jesus Christ : a guide for study and devotion / Alister E. McGrath.
    pages cm. -- (The heart of Christian faith series)
Includes bibliographical references.
ISBN 978-0-664-23908-4 (pbk : alk. paper) 1. Jesus Christ--Person and offices. I. Title.
BT203.M3399 2014
232--dc23

2014016543

Most Westminster John Knox Press books are available at special quantity
discounts when purchased in bulk by corporations, organizations, and special-interest
groups. For more information, please e-mail SpecialSales@wjkbooks.com.

Contents

Introduction

'I believe in Jesus Christ.' At the heart of the Christian faith lies not a set of abstract ideas or beliefs, but a *person* – one of the most attractive and intriguing figures the world has ever known.

Just as all roads in the ancient world led to Rome, so all Christian thinking about God and ourselves points us to the haunting figure of Jesus. The 'basic core' of the Christian faith is 'the beauty of the saving love of God made manifest in Jesus Christ who died and rose from the dead'.[1] Christians have always insisted that there is something special, something qualitatively different about Jesus. The New Testament makes plain that he is the lens through which we see God most clearly, and a mirror in which we can find ourselves reflected accurately and reliably. Through Jesus, we learn what God is like. But, just as importantly, we also learn what it really means to be human.

Even a casual glance at the Apostles' Creed or the Nicene Creed shows how central the figure of Jesus is to Christian life and thought. Both creeds devote more attention to him than to any other aspect of Christian belief. Why is this? Part of the answer, we shall discover, lies in the fact that Jesus Christ is both someone we know about, and the one who makes knowledge possible. He is the ground of our knowledge of God and, at the same time, the substance of our knowledge of God. He is, in short, the basis of our transformation and hope. 'The joy of the gospel fills the hearts and lives of all who encounter Jesus. Those who accept his offer of salvation are set free from sin, sorrow, inner emptiness and loneliness. With Christ joy is constantly born anew.'[2]

In the first volume in this series, we learned that the creeds have their origins partly in the personal confession of faith that early church converts made at the time of their baptism. Traditionally, Lent was seen as a period for instruction and reflection, with baptism taking place on Easter Day. Each candidate was asked three questions:

1 Do you believe in God, the Father Almighty?
2 Do you believe in Jesus Christ, the Son of God?
3 Do you believe in the Holy Spirit?

The creeds embody an expanded response to these three questions. But the answer that has been developed most fully concerns Jesus. The Apostles' Creed goes into some detail about the identity and significance of Jesus of Nazareth:

> I believe in Jesus Christ, God's only Son, our Lord, who was conceived by the Holy Spirit, born of the Virgin Mary, suffered under Pontius Pilate, was crucified, died, and was buried; he descended to the dead. On the third day he rose again; he ascended into heaven, he is seated at the right hand of the Father, and he will come to judge the living and the dead.

This crisp, confident summary allows Christians to affirm that Jesus of Nazareth is the Son of God, who entered into our history to die for our sins, and who rose again in triumph over both sin and death.

Some readers of this section of the creed may, however, feel rather uneasy. It seems to describe Jesus in much the same way as an historical textbook would tell us about Napoleon or George Washington. There is nothing, for example, about the personality of Jesus, which had such a powerful impact on those he encountered in the past, and which continues to inspire those he encounters today. The purpose of the creeds, though, is to provide us with a framework of meaning, a summary of key insights, which allow us to make more sense of who Jesus is, and why he matters. They are a brief expression of faith, a series of paragraph headings, not a comprehensive defence of its ideas or a rigorous exploration of its themes.

Other readers might find the creeds' emphasis on Jesus puzzling. Surely the important thing is to believe in God. Why this focus on an historical rather than on a transcendent figure? The answer to this important question is that 'God' can easily be understood in generalized and abstract terms. But Christianity is concerned with one very specific God – namely, 'the God and Father of our Lord Jesus Christ' – a god who entered history in a specific slice of place and time, which turns out to have universal significance.

Let's then begin to consider the rich and complex Christian understanding of the identity and significance of Jesus of Nazareth, which shapes our understanding of God.

Like the other volumes in this series, this book is based on sermons I preached over a number of years, and I would like to dedicate it once more with great affection to the people of the Shill Valley and Broadshire benefice in the diocese of Oxford, consisting of the churches in the Cotswold villages of Alvescot, Black Bourton, Broadwell, Broughton Poggs, Filkins, Holwell, Kelmscott, Kencot, Langford, Little Faringdon, Shilton and Westwell.

Alister McGrath

1

Jesus of Nazareth: the turning point

We all need heroes – people we can look up to, who inspire us to become better human beings. When I was very young, well-meaning relatives gave me lots of books about the history of the ancient world. As I began reading, I became fascinated by some of the great stories of the classical period. I was enchanted by Homer's *Odyssey* and its central character, Odysseus. But perhaps my greatest hero was Alexander the Great. I read the stories of his conquests with enormous enthusiasm: here was someone really interesting, who seemed to me to be a wonderful role model. It wasn't until I grew older that I realized there was a darker side to Alexander too.

Back in my youth, I assumed that Christians were people who looked up to Jesus of Nazareth, much as I hero-worshipped Alexander the Great. I personally found it difficult to see why! He was someone who had some good things to say, certainly, but it seemed to me that Christians had inflated his importance. They had added on a host of strange ideas which made it difficult to perceive him as any kind of role model, because the essence of a role model, I believed, was that he should be like me – only better. My heroes were people who made me want to imitate them.

So why on earth did Christianity talk about things like Jesus being 'truly divine'? That was making something very simple needlessly complicated. Christianity was surely about bringing our behaviour into line with the New Testament's account of the life and teachings of Jesus, who was a good religious and moral teacher – and no more. Christmas was merely the time of year when Christians remembered his birth, and Good Friday the day on which they remembered his death. As for Easter, I found it a total mystery.

As I reacted against religion in my late teens, it was inevitable that I would also react against Jesus. But though my hostility towards people who professed faith led me to view Jesus with suspicion, I couldn't help but be aware of his haunting, enigmatic quality. I had a nagging feeling that I was missing something, and couldn't quite work out what it was. There were other things to worry about in any case, like getting ready to study the natural sciences at Oxford University. So I stopped thinking about Jesus. And there I expected the matter to rest.

But it didn't. During my first term at Oxford, I gradually realized that atheism was drab and bleak, while Christianity was intellectually rich and vibrant. I still find it difficult to put into words what drew me to faith. Conversations with friends helped me grasp that I had misunderstood what Christianity was all about. I had the sense of standing on the shoreline of an immense ocean that stretched out as far as the eye could see, and like Evelyn Waugh before me (see the first book in this series, *Faith and the Creeds*, page 29), I began the delicious and delightful process of exploring my new-found faith. In time, I came to sense what was so special about Jesus of Nazareth, and in the following pages,

I would like to set out some of the ideas and approaches I found helpful, in the hope that they will be useful to you too.

It was the 1950s, and I was staying with my grandparents in their house in the Irish countryside. It was very cold. The windows in my bedroom had frosted over and I could see nothing through them. There were very beautiful, delicate patterns on the ice that covered the glass – whorls, stars and spirals – but they prevented me from observing what was outside. So I took a piece of cloth and began to rub the surface of the window. In a few moments, I had cleared enough to reveal what lay beyond: sparkling white hedges and fields, stretching far into the distance.

Everyone reading this book will be able to think of a similar story. Maybe you were struggling to focus a telescope when a fuzzy blur suddenly became a crisp and sharp landscape, or you remember a moment when confusing matters or events began to fall into a coherent pattern. It's as if someone turns a light on and you see how things hang together for the first time. There are lots of occasions when we simply can't quite work out how everything fits together. We need someone to tell us. Or to show us.

That's the human predicament. Living in a world of swirling mist, of shadows and half-light, we know deep down that there is a God and long to know what this God is *really* like. The Psalmist put it brilliantly, when he expressed his deep yearning to 'see the goodness of the LORD in the land of the living' (Psalm 27.13), and this same idea is expressed time after time in the Old Testament.

The people of Israel knew there was a God. They called this God by name – the 'Lord God of Israel'. This was a faithful God, who could be trusted, whose glory was reflected in the beauty and majesty of the natural world. Yet this God often seemed distant from everyday existence, and perhaps this helps us understand why Israel longed for their God to come close – to visit them.

The last prophetic work of the Old Testament, the book of Malachi, expresses this longing of Israel in words that are both beautiful and heart-rending: 'the Lord whom you seek will suddenly come to his temple' (Malachi 3.1). But as the centuries pass, nothing seems to happen. The God who is the heart's desire of Israel never comes. Perhaps God has forgotten Israel. Or perhaps there is no God to forget Israel in the first place.

Then everything changes. Something *happens*. And afterwards, for those who are aware of its significance, the world becomes very different. The New Testament and the creeds leave us in no doubt about what this event is – the life, death and resurrection of Jesus of Nazareth.

The story of Jesus of Nazareth

Stories engage our imagination, often opening up deeper and better ways of thinking for us to explore. The story of Jesus of Nazareth is perhaps the greatest and most engaging story ever told. The four Gospels set out to tell that story and by doing so give rise to ideas about Jesus – ideas that are affirmed and examined more thoroughly in early Christian preaching (in the Acts of the Apostles) and teaching (mainly in the New Testament letters).

The story of Jesus cannot be told in isolation but rather links up with other stories: one concerns God's creation of the world; another tells of God's calling of Israel; a third tells of the age-old human quest for meaning and significance. The story of Jesus intersects with all three. His is the story that allows us to see all other stories in their proper light. Greek philosophy and the law of Israel alike were fulfilled and transcended in this one individual, who declares, 'Do not think that I have come to abolish the law or the prophets; I have come not to abolish but to fulfil' (Matthew 5.17). Human wisdom and divine promise converge in Jesus of Nazareth.

The Gospel of Mark, which we will turn to frequently in this chapter, quickly draws our attention to the figure of John the Baptist, and makes a connection between the appearance of John and the great prophetic expectation of the coming of the Lord. 'See, I am sending my messenger ahead of you, who will prepare your way; the voice of one crying out in the wilderness: "Prepare the way of the Lord"' (Mark 1.2–3). John is a transitional figure between the Old Covenant and the New, pointing to someone even more significant who will come after him (Mark 1.7–8). 'In those days Jesus came from Nazareth in Galilee and was baptized by John in the Jordan' (Mark 1.9).

Mark's story of Jesus of Nazareth continues with his account of the calling of the first disciples.

> As Jesus passed along the Sea of Galilee, he saw Simon and his brother Andrew casting a net into the lake – for they were fishermen. And Jesus said to them, 'Follow me and I will make you fish for people.' And immediately they left their nets and followed him.   (Mark 1.16–18)

Those first disciples clearly found something compelling in Jesus – a sort of 'X factor' that could never be put into words. Perhaps they did not fully understand their own reasons for following him. But we are left in no doubt that they recognized that there was something very special about this stranger. So powerful was his attraction that they left behind their nets – their only source of income as fishermen.

The theme of deep personal trust in Jesus of Nazareth runs through the long history of Christian thought. People find in him something transformative and satisfying – a reason for living, their heart's desire, a firm stronghold in times of despair, or someone who seems to know the secrets of the kingdom of God. Without fully understanding who Jesus is, or why he should be so compelling, they choose to follow him. Their hearts have been won. Their imaginations have been captivated. Their minds, however, must now try to take in what has happened. Who must Jesus be to elicit such a response on their part? What is so different about him? They are following Jesus; they have yet to figure out just who he is.

I found myself reading and rereading that passage, Mark 1.16–18, in my first period of faith. After reading it, I felt I had glimpsed something only partially, yet with sufficient clarity to want to know more, and to trust that there was more to be known. I felt like someone on the brow of a hill, looking down over a shrouded landscape, patiently waiting for the mist to lift. And as I continued to read Mark's Gospel, I began to appreciate that the disciples seem to have been in a similar position to my own. They didn't really understand who Jesus of Nazareth was either. They recognized that there was something very special about him – the aforementioned 'X factor' – but realized there was yet much to discover. Gradually, they began to learn more about the identity and significance of Jesus, and as I journeyed with them, reading Mark's Gospel, I shared in their discoveries.

It is almost as if Mark is gradually drawing aside a curtain, so his readers are allowed to see Jesus of Nazareth just a bit at a time. It would be impossible for someone to take in everything about Jesus at once, so once we've appreciated a particular aspect of his significance, Mark moves us on. Jesus' character is revealed, layer by layer, each adding depth and detail to what we already know. And through living in Jesus' company, we gradually grow in our understanding of what he is all about.

Looking back on my days as a student, I now realize that I had some of the best teachers I could have hoped for. I recall a lecturer at Oxford who introduced us to quantum theory – one of the most important (and difficult) aspects of modern physics. He began by asking us to think of atoms being like tiny suns with planets orbiting them. We all nodded in agreement. That seemed very straightforward. Atoms had nuclei (which were like the sun) and electrons (which were like the planets). The lecturer played around with the mathematics till he was sure we'd understood him. It all seemed so easy.

Then he smiled at us in a rather apologetic manner. 'Actually, it's a bit more complicated than that.' And he began to explain how we needed to modify this very simple picture in order to fit in the experimental results. But he explained it so well that we were able to follow him. And once he was sure we had understood this more complex model, he smiled again. 'Actually, it's a bit more complicated than that as well . . .'

By the end of the course, we had been brought up to speed with the latest thinking in this hugely complex area of scientific thought. Something that seemed to be simple turned out to be much more complicated, exciting and satisfying. But by leading us into it gradually, step by step and layer by layer, our lecturer helped us to build up the rich picture of reality disclosed by quantum theory.

That's exactly what theologians found to be true about the identity of Jesus of Nazareth. We begin by thinking of him in very simple terms – for example, as our Lord, our friend, or our redeemer. And once we've worked out what that means, we realize that it's a bit more complicated than that. It's all about stretching our minds and hearts, so that we can grasp Jesus of Nazareth in all his fullness, instead of being satisfied with slick and easy answers to deep and important questions.

Let's try and tease out some of the themes that we find in Mark's narrative. We'll begin with one we've already begun to explore, which is evident in the calling of the first disciples, and echoed in many of the accounts of the encounters of Jesus with others. There was something special about him – something that fascinated people, compelling them to pay attention, drawing them in, and ultimately leading them to follow him.

For many of us, given our over-intellectualized Western culture, this seems to make little sense. Surely we ought to work out who Jesus really is before we throw caution to the winds? Surely rational reflection ought to come before personal commitment? Yet Mark's account of the impact of Jesus on those around him offers another way of looking at things. There seems to be something about Jesus that invites a response at the deepest level of our being. We know the disciples realized they were in the presence of someone rather special and that their decision to follow him included a commitment to work out what it was that made him so. Their personal commitment to Jesus of Nazareth led to an extended 'discipleship of the mind', as their heads tried to catch up with their hearts.

It's hard to find an analogy that does justice to this aspect of Jesus, as depicted in the Gospels, but a good attempt at expressing it may be seen in C. S. Lewis's character Aslan, the great lion of Narnia. Lewis presents Aslan as a 'Christ-figure', a literary figure who in some way echoes and embodies the presence and person of Jesus of Nazareth. Throughout the Chronicles of Narnia, Lewis portrays Aslan as a magnificent and noble lion, who has a profound impact on those he meets, including the four Pevensie children, who have found their way into Narnia through the famous wardrobe in the old Professor's house. Aslan evokes *awe and wonder*. He is *wild* – an awe-inspiring, magnificent creature, who has not been tamed through domestication, or had his claws pulled out to ensure he is powerless. When his name is mentioned for the first time, the four children feel 'quite different'. Yet they have dissimilar reactions. Edmund feels 'mysterious horror'; Peter feels 'brave and adventurous'; Susan feels elated; and Lucy gets the feeling you have when you 'realize it is the beginning of the holidays'.[1]

There is clearly something special about Aslan. *Each of the children experiences him in his or her own distinct way.* The one Aslan relates to each child in a special way – a way that reflects his identity and their own. Lewis's narrative, widely regarded as one of the finest expressions of Christianity's respect for the individuality of believers, constantly emphasizes that Aslan encounters and transforms people individually. They want to know more about him because they find him so enthralling and majestic. It is impossible to miss Lewis's allusions to the Gospel narratives about the encounters between Jesus Christ and individuals – such as Zacchaeus or the woman at the well. Such individuals come away from those encounters as different people. Their world has been turned upside down by a stranger who seems to know everything about them. And having encountered him and been amazed by him, they try to work out who he really is.

We'll revisit this theme of the deep attractiveness of Jesus later in this book. For the moment, let's return to Mark's account and consider another strand of his story – that of Jesus of Nazareth as teacher.

More than just a teacher

We are all familiar with the figure of a teacher – a person who says things we believe to be helpful, valuable and reliable. Mark tells us that many crowded around Jesus to hear his parables of the kingdom of God, while making clear that there was something unusual about the quality of Jesus' words. 'They were astounded at his teaching, for he taught them as one having authority' (Mark 1.22).

This is probably the aspect of Jesus we find easiest to understand. Mark obviously wants us to reflect on Jesus' qualities as a teacher. Why was he so authoritative? Was it that he taught very effectively? Or did people perceive an extraordinary depth in him, something that set Jesus apart from other religious teachers of his day?

It's an important question, so let's pause for a moment to think it through. There is no doubt that Jesus was a religious teacher. The problem is that some people limit his significance to this single category in an effort to solve the riddle of his identity. Well, Jesus being a teacher is part of the truth, but it's not the whole truth. It's a snapshot, but not the 'big picture'. His role cannot be limited to giving us good advice, for that would make us people whose only need was to be told what to do. And just as there's no point in advising a blind woman that she ought to learn to see, there's little point in telling us the good deeds we ought to perform if there's actually something wrong with human nature that prevents us from doing the good we wish to! We need healing and renewal, not merely words of wisdom. We need to be enabled to do good, not just told what to do.

As the creeds make clear, Christians do not view Jesus as merely a rabbi, but as their Lord and Saviour. They talk about Jesus being the 'Bread of Life', or the 'Lamb of God, who takes away the sin of the world'. We will undoubtedly value Jesus' moral teaching, but our main interest concerns the significance of his death and resurrection. Good teachers, after all, are not that difficult to find; people who are crucified, only to be raised from the dead are rather fewer on the ground, and command attention for that very reason.

But let's rejoin Mark as he continues to relate the story of Jesus of Nazareth.

Jesus the healer and forgiver

One incident which took place very early in his ministry is particularly important in helping us to put together the 'big picture' about Jesus – the healing of a paralytic (Mark 2.1–12). The Gospels make clear that Jesus of Nazareth had a healing ministry, which drew many to hear him speak. Healing is about restoration to wholeness. While important in itself, healing can be seen as an analogy for the whole process of salvation – restoring creation and humanity to what God wanted them to be.

But let's focus on this single event, as there is a deeper point to be made. Mark paints a vivid picture of the scene, helping us to sense its drama. Jesus had drawn large crowds on account of his healing ministry. Hearing that he was in their neighbourhood, four people attempted to bring their paralysed friend to him.

But they couldn't get near Jesus because of the mass of people. Undeterred, they climbed on the roof of the building in which Jesus was staying, and lowered their friend onto the floor inside. We'll let Mark take up the story.

> When Jesus saw their faith, he said to the paralytic, 'Son, your sins are forgiven.' Now some of the scribes were sitting there, questioning in their hearts, 'Why does this fellow speak in this way? It is blasphemy! Who can forgive sins but God alone?' (Mark 2.5–7)

It is easy for us to fail to appreciate the drama of the moment when Jesus declared that the man's sins were forgiven. Yet everyone who heard those words knew their deeper significance. Every good Jew was aware that only God can forgive sins. The 'scribes' – the experts in the Jewish law – were quite right. Through what he said, Jesus was claiming to be able to do something – forgive sins – that only God could do. Jesus was thus guilty of blasphemy. Unless, that is, the unthinkable, the unimaginable, were actually true. Unless – however strange this might seem – Jesus really was God, though that seemed simply inconceivable within the thinking of orthodox Judaism at that time.

What happens next in Mark's story? Jesus' words to the paralytic actually tell us rather a lot about Jesus himself.

> 'But so that you may know that the Son of Man has authority on earth to forgive sins' – he said to the paralytic – 'I say to you, stand up, take your mat and go to your home.' And he stood up, and immediately took the mat and went out before all of them; so that they were all amazed and glorified God, saying, 'We have never seen anything like this!'
>
> (Mark 2.10–12)

It is little wonder the crowds were astonished as they realized the implications of what they had just seen and heard. Someone had claimed authority to act as God and for God. And far from striking Jesus dead by a thunderbolt from heaven, God appeared to have honoured – even endorsed – this astonishing claim. What could it mean? Did this imply that Jesus was able to do things that only God was able to do? And if so, what ramifications did that have for his identity?

As Mark's narrative progresses, more pieces are added to the jigsaw. The first disciples accompany Jesus on his ministry, and gradually begin to grasp his significance. They listen to what he says, and watch what he does. And some – but not yet all – of the bits of the puzzle begin to fall into place. For example, Mark tells the story of how Jesus was able to still the storms on the Sea of Galilee, to the amazement of the disciples. 'They were filled with great awe, and said to one another, "Who then is this, that even the wind and the sea obey him?"' (Mark 4.35–41). What were the implications of Jesus' actions in terms of his identity? Who was Jesus, if he was able to do these things?

The crucifixion of Jesus of Nazareth

As Mark continues his story, the mood darkens. Jesus draws near to Jerusalem, and is welcomed by the crowds as if he were a conquering hero. Yet he is betrayed to the Roman and Jewish authorities, and condemned to be crucified.

The Gospel accounts of the death of Jesus on a cross on the first Good Friday are deeply moving. We are left in no doubt that he suffered a slow and lingering death, with devastating results for his disciples. They were left bereft, hopeless and helpless, as Jesus died in front of their eyes and their world fell to pieces. Even Peter, supposedly the leader of the disciples, ended up denying any association with Jesus.

It is important to realize that Mark's Gospel shows no sign of hostility towards either the Jewish high priest Caiaphas or the Roman governor Pontius Pilate, as it relates how Jesus was brought before both to face condemnation. There is no place in Christianity for scapegoating any individual or group for the death of Christ. The Church has always insisted, and rightly, that the ultimate cause of his Passion was flawed and fallen human nature – something in which we all share. It is not a particularly pleasant or reassuring thought. We, it turns out, are the ones who are really being judged at the trial of Jesus of Nazareth.

The theme of Christ's crucifixion is deeply embedded in the New Testament, and one of the earliest literary witnesses to its central importance is Paul's first letter to the Christian church at Corinth. The letter probably dates from the early months of AD 54. In its first chapter, Paul lays considerable emphasis upon the fact that Jesus was crucified, even suggesting that the entire gospel could be summarized as 'the message about the cross' (1 Corinthians 1.18).

Crucifixion was seen by the Roman authorities as a humiliating and painful form of death, designed to deter anyone from thinking of attempting to subvert its authority. It is impossible to define what form a 'normal' crucifixion might take: the victim was generally flogged or tortured beforehand, and then might be tied or nailed to the cross in practically any position, subject only to the ingenuity and perversity of the executioner. Far from being an essentially bloodless form of execution, as some commentators have suggested, the victim is likely to have bled profusely. Only if he had not been flogged or tortured previously, and bound, rather than nailed to the cross, would no blood have been spilled.

This form of punishment appears to have been employed ruthlessly to suppress rebellions in the Roman provinces, such as the revolt of the Cantabrians in northern Spain, as well as the rebellions of the Jews. Josephus' accounts of the crucifixion of countless Jewish fugitives, who attempted to escape from besieged Jerusalem at the time of its final destruction by Roman armies, make horrifying reading. In the view of most Roman jurists, notorious criminals should be crucified on the exact location of their crime, so that 'the sight might deter others from such crimes'.[2]

Perhaps for this reason, the Roman emperor Quintillus crucified criminals on the busiest thoroughfares, in order that the maximum effect might be achieved. Some six thousand slaves who had rebelled against Rome under the leadership of Spartacus were crucified along the sides of the Appian Way – a major transport route – in 71 BC.

The death of Jesus on a cross was thus seen as enormously shameful, and the idea of a crucified saviour was seized upon by opponents of the early Church as demonstrating the ridiculous nature of Christian claims. The great Roman orator Marcus Cornelius Fronto declared that 'the religion of the Christians is insane, in that they worship a crucified man, and even the instrument of his punishment itself.'

Yet Christian writers never downplayed the crucifixion, despite this negative reaction within Roman culture. They clearly regarded it as central to the gospel proclamation. Let's look at three themes that are woven into the Gospel accounts of the crucifixion, and the New Testament's reflections on the meaning of that event.

First, it was humiliating and painful. Crucifixion ensured a slow, lingering death. Nobody wanted to die like that. That was what the Romans counted on. It was an inhumane means of execution, designed to discourage insurrection and rebellion. The New Testament makes it clear that Jesus of Nazareth died in the most degrading and painful manner known to humanity. *And he did this for us.*

As I reflect on the Gospel Passion accounts, I often find myself lingering over one particular scene. The crowds around the cross ridicule Jesus. 'Save yourself, and come down from the cross' (Mark 15.30). But he doesn't. He stays there, and saves us instead.

Second, we need to realize that there was a religious aspect to crucifixion. For a Jew, anyone hanged upon a tree was cursed by God (Deuteronomy 21.23). Indeed, one of the Dead Sea Scrolls suggests that crucifixion was regarded as the proper form of execution for a Jew suspected of high treason. This seemed to undermine any Christian claim that Jesus could be the long-awaited Messiah. The idea of a 'crucified Messiah' was a contradiction in terms. To die on a cross was to die under the curse of God. No wonder Jews saw crucifixion as such a shocking form of execution. To be put to death was bad enough. But to be executed in a manner that cut them off from God was unbearable.

Paul realized the importance of this point, and its relevance for the meaning of the cross. 'Christ redeemed us from the curse of the law by becoming a curse for us – for it is written, "Cursed is everyone who hangs on a tree"' (Galatians 3.13). By being crucified, Christ did indeed bear a curse – *our* curse, which he willingly bore.

And third, as we have already observed, the cross was seen by Roman society as a symbol of shame and weakness.

Roman critics of Christianity ridiculed its emphasis on the cross. This can be seen in the famous 'Alexamenos Graffito', found during some excavations near the Palatine Hill in Rome, and thought to date from the third century. This depicts a man bowing before a crucified human figure with the head of a donkey. Beneath it is written 'Alexamenos worships [his] God'.

Even in the New Testament itself, we see an awareness of a negative cultural reaction to its central idea of a 'crucified Messiah'. Paul argued that the weakness and 'folly' of the cross pointed to the strength and wisdom of God. The Jews expected the Messiah to be a triumphant conqueror; the Greeks wanted someone who was wise. Yet at the heart of the Christian faith was a crucified Messiah, who endured suffering in order to save. 'We proclaim Christ crucified, a stumbling-block to Jews and foolishness to Gentiles' (1 Corinthians 1.23).

The creeds make clear that the historical reality of the crucifixion matters. But the Christian faith is about more than what happened in the past. It's about the meaning of events. What difference does the crucifixion make? Why is it of such importance?

Let's recall one of Paul's fundamental statements to the church at Corinth: 'For I handed on to you as of first importance what I in turn had received: that Christ died for our sins in accordance with the scriptures' (1 Corinthians 15.3). Paul passes on to his readers in the great port city of Corinth what had originally been passed on to him – a compact summary of the core themes of the Christian faith. Paul takes an historical event – the death of Jesus – and adds on to this a layer of interpretation. Jesus did not just die; he died for our sins.

Events need explaining. We have to know what they mean – if, that is, they mean anything at all. Let's look at a textbook example, and tease this point out. Julius Caesar is probably one of the best-known figures in Roman history. In January 49 BC, he led an army southwards from northern Italy towards Rome. At one point, the army crossed the River Rubicon. By all accounts, it was not a large river, and it is doubtful whether Caesar's men had any difficulty getting from one side to the other. Crossing the river was not a monumental achievement, to be compared to climbing Mount Everest!

But that's not why we remember the crossing of the Rubicon. The reason this event has gone down in history is because the action had a deeper meaning. The Rubicon marked the border between northern Italian territory and the territories of Rome itself. By crossing the river with an army without official authorization, Julius Caesar had declared war on the senate and people of Rome. His words 'The die is cast!' reflect his awareness of the step he had just taken. There was no going back. If he failed, he would be punished by death. In the end, Caesar ended up as the victor in the civil war which broke out as a result of his act of rebellion.

Notice how the event is given its meaning by its context. If you or I were to cross the Rubicon today, it would not have the same significance. Context shapes meaning. That's why we need to take Paul's second point into account. Christ died for our sins *according to the scriptures*. What does this signify?

There are two things to note. First, that the death of Jesus on the cross was not an accident, but something that was somehow *meant* to happen, without in any way undermining the fact that Jesus freely chose to act in this way. 'Thus it is written, that the Messiah is to suffer and to rise from the dead on the third day' (Luke 24.46). Second, that we are meant to make sense of these events within a biblical framework. The death and resurrection of Jesus are to be seen as the fulfilment of prophecy, and to be interpreted against the Old Testament's understanding of the significance of sin and how God might deal with it.

Later we shall look at what are sometimes called 'theories of the atonement' – ways of trying to make sense of the meaning of the death of Jesus on the cross in order to appreciate its full significance. But for now we'll let Mark tell us more of the story of Jesus of Nazareth. We know he died on the cross . . . What happened next?

The resurrection of Jesus of Nazareth

The solemn recollection of the death of Jesus in the Apostles' Creed is immediately followed by a dramatic, upbeat declaration of the total transformation of the situation. 'On the third day he rose again.' We can only guess at the emotion of the occasion, as the first disciples realized that the one they loved and followed had been restored to them. Sorrow must have been replaced, first by disbelief, then by exultation, and finally by reflection on what all this meant.

J. R. R. Tolkien coined the word 'eucatastrophe' to refer to the moment in which despair is utterly transformed and gives way to joy. What seemed like a defeat becomes instead a moment of deliverance. Tolkien had no doubt what the supreme example of a 'eucatastrophe' was – the resurrection of Jesus, which allowed the disciples to catch a 'fleeting glimpse' of a 'Joy beyond the walls of the world'.[3] This 'sudden and miraculous grace' totally changes the story, making our hearts beat faster as we realize that something momentous has happened and try to take it in. In a pattern characteristic of the New Testament, death leads to new life; despair leads to hope; suffering leads to glory.

The New Testament treats the resurrection as a 'sign' – an outward event, with a deeper inward meaning. Part of the New Testament proclamation of the resurrection concerns the empty tomb. But that is the outer shell of history; within it lies a precious pearl of meaning. Sometimes Christians get fixated on proving the historical reliability of the accounts of the empty tomb. But that's only part of the picture. When the New Testament talks about 'resurrection', it means a lot more than an empty tomb.

Some argue that the ancient world was full of stories about dying and rising gods, such as Egyptian vegetation deities, who 'died' in the winter and were 'born again' in the spring, and that Christians just borrowed these ideas. Yet the first Christians don't seem to have known anything about these. The resurrection of Jesus of Nazareth has nothing to do with the disappearance and reappearance of grass! The first Christians were confronted with a series of historical events which needed interpretation – such as an empty tomb. What did this mean?

Others argue that the resurrection had to be an invention. These things just don't happen. Yet this is to rule out any unique events within history as a matter of principle. G. K. Chesterton put the point rather well: 'The believers in miracles accept them (rightly or wrongly) because they have evidence for them. The disbelievers in miracles deny them (rightly or wrongly) because they have a doctrine against them.'[4] Chesterton was surely right: a dogmatic belief that miracles cannot happen leads some people to refuse to take the resurrection seriously. The 'principle of analogy' (the belief that what happened in the past mirrors what happens in the present) is useful as an historical tool. It can tell us when something unusual has happened. But it's unreliable as a view of reality. It encounters serious difficulties when it tries to tell us what can – and cannot – have happened.

Suppose that resurrections happened all the time. Would we have difficulty in believing that Jesus was raised? No. But would it be *significant*? No. It would be an everyday event, lacking any special quality. The critical point is that the importance of an historical event is directly proportional to its rarity. The New Testament makes it clear that the resurrection of Jesus of Nazareth was unexpected, without any parallel in history.

It might be suggested that Christians just took over some Jewish ideas here. Yet this is not easy to argue in the face of the evidence. For a start, most Jews believed in a general resurrection *at the end of time*, when history came to an end, not in a resurrection *within* human history. There's also a major difference in the importance attached to the idea of resurrection. In what scholars call 'second-Temple Judaism' – that is, the forms of Judaism that developed after the return from exile in Babylon – the idea of resurrection is certainly seen as important. But it's not seen as *central*. Many works written in this period make no reference to the idea. But the New Testament sees resurrection as being of defining importance.

Mark's account of the resurrection opens by telling us how three women visited the tomb on the Sunday morning. 'Mary Magdalene, and Mary the mother of James, and Salome bought spices, so that they might go and anoint him' (Mark 16.1).

Clearly, the intention was to treat the corpse of the beloved Jesus with the respect and reverence he deserved. Despite the fact that the testimony of a woman was held to be of no consequence in the patriarchal society of his day, Mark makes no attempt to alter the facts so they seem more credible. The two Marys and Salome were confronted with something they were not expecting, which utterly confused them. Was it a trick of the early morning light? The tomb seemed to be empty.

We might expect the women to have been overjoyed, perhaps shattering the early morning stillness with shouts of 'Alleluia! Jesus is risen!' But Mark conveys that the vocabulary of joy is absent. The women were seized with 'terror and amazement', reduced to silence, and impelled to flight (Mark 16.5–8). The kind of fearful reverence we read about here is like that of Moses in his encounter with God at the burning bush, which led to his commissioning to lead Israel out of Egypt into the Promised Land (Exodus 3.6). The shepherds in the fields around Bethlehem who witnessed the angels were likewise terrified (Luke 2.9–10); they were overwhelmed by the glory of God.

As we have seen, this dramatic new turn in the story of Jesus of Nazareth did not fit into any existing Jewish way of thinking. Though most Jews of the time seem to have believed in a general resurrection that would take place right at the end of history, nobody believed in a resurrection in the here and now, in the world of time and space, in front of witnesses. Far from endorsing existing expectations, it demanded their reconsideration. It was a game-changer, something that the old wineskins of first-century Judaism just couldn't accommodate.

It was when I was studying the history of science at Oxford that I first came across the idea of a 'paradigm shift'. This phrase was invented by Thomas Kuhn, who used it to describe a seismic shift in scientific thinking, when the evidence demands a new way of seeing things. Back in the Middle Ages, most people believed the sun orbited the earth. As more precise observations built up, there came a tipping point when the old way of thinking could no longer be sustained. A new approach had to be developed. The evidence demanded it.

The resurrection of Jesus of Nazareth may be said to have caused a 'paradigm shift' to take place within the first community of Christians. The old ways of thinking just couldn't cope with what had been experienced. New ways of thinking about things had to be found. This process can be seen happening in the story of the Road to Emmaus (Luke 24.13–31). Two followers of Jesus of Nazareth are walking towards the village of Emmaus, discussing the wild rumours that are circulating about what happened to him. They are joined by a stranger, who asks what they have been talking about.

They tell their travelling companion that they have been discussing Jesus, who was, according to Jewish thinking, 'a prophet mighty in deed and word before God and all the people' and 'the one to redeem Israel' (24.19, 21). Yet the rumours sweeping across Judaea call this into question. If it is true that Jesus has risen from the dead, then he is far more than those existing Jewish categories suggested or permitted.

Then the stranger begins to speak to them. He tells them Israel's story: 'beginning with Moses and all the prophets, he interpreted to them the things about himself in all the scriptures' (24.27). He offers a new way of making sense of Israel's history and a new way of locating and interpreting a vital part of that great narrative – the story of Jesus himself. This is not a tale about another failed messianic uprising, routed by the Roman authorities. Rather, it tells of a new era in the history of God's dealings with his people and with the world. 'Was it not necessary that the Messiah should suffer these things and then enter into his glory?' (24.26) The two followers have been trying to unlock the meaning of recent history using the wrong key. And as they walk, a new key is slowly but surely turned and a door opens into a new way of understanding what is going on. A paradigm shift is taking place, and a new way of thinking is in the process of crystallizing.

Once more, we realize that the resurrection is something that needs to be interpreted. It gives a new turn – and a new meaning – to the story of Jesus of Nazareth. It also gives a new direction to the story of people's lives. In the next chapter, we will reflect on this in greater detail.

2

Jesus of Nazareth: assembling the big picture

I was staying with some colleagues in Yorkshire, in the north of England. One evening we went to a nearby restaurant for a meal. A few moments after we had returned home for a cup of tea, a car pulled up outside. One of my colleagues looked out the window to see who our visitor might be. 'Oh no! It's Mr Bore and Snore!' he whispered. The others put their heads in their hands. 'Pretend we're not here!' someone suggested. But it was too late.

It didn't take me long to work out how the new arrival had acquired his nickname. After giving us an utterly tedious lecture on the economics of the insurance business, he settled down in the most comfortable chair and fell asleep. And snored. In fact, he snored so loudly, we had to move to another room so that we could hear each other speak. This encounter has reminded me ever since that the names we give people tell us a lot about what we think of them.

Names really mattered to the biblical writers. They were seen as expressing who someone was, while being allowed to name someone indicated you had authority over them. In the creation accounts, Adam is allowed to name the animals (Genesis 2.19–20) because they come under his stewardship.

And when Daniel and his companions are exiled to Babylon, they are given new names to indicate they are servants of the state (Daniel 1.7).

But no human being is allowed to give a name to God, as this would imply that we have some kind of authority over God. This point is made clearly in several passages in the Old Testament. Moses wants to know the name by which the God of Abraham, Isaac and Jacob is to be known. And God tells him what name he is to use.

> Moses said to God, 'If I come to the Israelites and say to them, "The God of your ancestors has sent me to you", and they ask me, "What is his name?", what shall I say to them?' God said to Moses, 'I AM WHO I AM.' (Exodus 3.13–14)

In the same way, Mary and Joseph are not allowed to choose the name of their child. 'Jesus' is an anglicized version of *Iesous*, the Greek form of the Hebrew name *Yeshua* which literally means 'God saves'. But the idea of Jesus as a potential saviour was not his earthly parents' idea. The name was chosen for them and they were authorized to give it to the child, with all it would imply.

Let's now explore the three particular titles used to describe Jesus in the body of the Apostles' Creed: 'I believe in Jesus Christ, [God's] only Son, our Lord.' We must not see these three titles – or any others, for that matter – as prisons, designed to trap our thought. Rather, they are the wellspring of reflection, in which our minds, imaginations and hearts are opened up to the richness and joy of God. Pope Francis has reminded Christians how easily we can limit Jesus, reducing him to neat little theological categories. Jesus transcends these. He cannot be imprisoned in a theoretical cage!

Jesus can also break through the dull categories with which we would enclose him and he constantly amazes us by his divine creativity. Whenever we make the effort to return to the source and to recover the original freshness of the Gospel, new avenues arise, new paths of creativity open up, with different forms of expression, more eloquent signs and words with new meaning for today's world.[1]

To appreciate Jesus to the full, we need to avoid trapping him in our preconceived categories, which, like old wineskins, are simply not capable of holding him. With this point in mind, let us begin to explore these titles, beginning with Jesus as the 'Messiah'.

Jesus the Messiah

'I believe in Jesus Christ'. Most of us treat the name 'Jesus Christ' as if it were a forename and surname – like John Doe or Mary Smith. But it's not. It's a title: 'Jesus the Messiah'. The Greek word *Christos* is a translation of the Hebrew word 'Messiah', and this term is deeply rooted in the history and hopes of the people of Israel. Literally, it means 'the anointed one' – someone who has been ceremonially anointed with oil in recognition of being endowed by God with special powers and functions. From the outset, the idea of the Messiah was associated with the king, first of all with Saul and then with David. After David's death, the Messiah increasingly became understood as his successor, someone who would restore Israel to the golden age she had enjoyed under the rule of her greatest leader.

So when would the Messiah come? There seems little doubt that some believed this would happen when the people of Jerusalem returned to Judah after the long period of exile in

Babylon. The restoration of the nation of Israel after its long period of exile seemed to suggest that it was on the brink of a new messianic age. We can catch something of this sense of anticipation as we read the great prophecies of deliverance spoken to the exiled people of Jerusalem as they languished in Babylon, hardly daring to hope that they might one day return home.

> Comfort, O comfort my people, says your God.
> Speak tenderly to Jerusalem, and cry to her that she
>   has served her term, that her penalty is paid, that
>   she has received from the LORD's hand double for
>   all her sins.
> A voice cries out: 'In the wilderness prepare the way
>   of the LORD, make straight in the desert a highway
>   for our God.
> Every valley shall be lifted up, and every mountain
>   and hill be made low; the uneven ground shall
>   become level, and the rough places a plain.'
>
> (Isaiah 40.1–4)

The people of Jerusalem did indeed return home, as the military and political power of Babylon collapsed. But the Messiah did not come. Things began to go badly wrong. The post-exilic community gradually realized that the prophetic ideals of restoration had not been met and that the coming of the promised Messiah still lay in the future. But when? And how would they know when to expect his coming?

That's why the appearance of John the Baptist was seen as a turning point. According to the prophets, the coming of God to visit and redeem Israel would be signalled by the advent of a messenger – a trailblazer, who would prepare the way for the coming of the Messiah. 'I am sending my messenger to prepare the way before me, and the Lord whom you seek will suddenly come to his temple' (Malachi 3.1). When John the Baptist appeared in the wilderness, proclaiming the need for national repentance, he created a sensation. Vast crowds flocked to see and hear him.

Yet the appeal of John lay only partly in his message of repentance. More importantly, he declared that he was a herald, preparing the way for the coming of someone much greater than himself. 'The one who is more powerful than I is coming after me; I am not worthy to stoop down and untie the thong of his sandals. I have baptized you with water; but he will baptize you with the Holy Spirit' (Mark 1.7–8). So who is this mysterious figure? As if anticipating our question, Mark answers it: 'In those days Jesus came from Nazareth of Galilee and was baptized by John in the Jordan' (Mark 1.9).

Jesus' ministry took place in the Roman province of Judaea, when fierce nationalist feeling, fuelled by hostility towards the foreign occupying power, seems to have reignited the traditional expectation of the coming of the Messiah. For many, the Messiah would be the deliverer who expelled the Romans, returned Israel to the rightful rule of the Jewish people and restored the line of David.

Jesus of Nazareth seems to have been regarded by some in this political way. The Gospels vividly describe his reception as he entered the city of Jerusalem on what we now call Palm Sunday: the crowds who gathered round him used language and actions – such as strewing the ground with palm branches – appropriate for the coming of a triumphant warrior king.

But Jesus did not see himself as Messiah in this political sense. At no point in his ministry do we find him urging violence or opposition against Rome. Indeed, his criticisms are usually directed primarily against his own people and their failure to honour God. Thus after his triumphal entry into Jerusalem (Matthew 21.8–11), which seems to be a deliberate messianic gesture, Jesus immediately evicts the money-changers from the temple (Matthew 21.12–13). His concern was to renew and redirect the obedience and faith of Israel towards God.

Furthermore, Jesus was not prepared to accept the title 'Messiah' in public in the course of his ministry. Mark's Gospel should be read carefully to note this point. When Peter acclaims Jesus as Messiah, Jesus immediately tells him to keep quiet about it (8.29–30). He then explains to his disciples that he must suffer, be rejected by his own people and killed. This is not the kind of Messiah that Israel is expecting! The Jews longed for a conquering king; they did not imagine for a moment that their Messiah would be executed as a common criminal.

Why do we continue to speak of Jesus as 'Christ' – the Messiah? Some scholars suggest that, as Christianity expanded in the Roman world and the roots of the faith in Judaism gradually faded from memory, the word 'Christ' may have lost much of its original meaning and become a kind of shorthand for 'Jesus of Nazareth'. 'Jesus Christ' became a name like 'John Smith' or 'Jane Doe'. 'Christ' was understood as a surname, not as a title.

However, the creeds make it clear that Jesus of Nazareth cannot be fully understood without reference to the history of Israel. The God of Jesus of Nazareth is the same as the God of Abraham, Isaac and Jacob. This point is emphasized in the letter to the Hebrews, which showcases the great figures of faith of the Old Testament. Jesus represents the point of transition from what was a national religion to a universal faith. Christians see things more clearly on account of Jesus of Nazareth than our Old Testament forebears did; we are able to receive and possess what was merely hinted at in the past history of the people of God. We are privileged to enter into the inheritance which the great figures of faith in the past greeted and welcomed 'from a distance'.

Jesus the Son of God

The creeds move on, and invite us to believe also in Jesus as 'God's only Son'. Behind this declaration lies a powerful and energizing vision of a God who does not stand above human history, but enters into it in an engaging and transformational way. Above all, God enters the world in personal form – not as an abstract idea or an invisible force.

Of course, referring to Jesus as the 'Son of God' does more than affirm that *Jesus is like God*: it also makes clear that *God is like Jesus*. Our God is not one who is hidden from us, as some inscrutable and distant despot. Rather God's will is made known and his face shown in Jesus of Nazareth. The creeds reassure us that Jesus is the gateway through which we have access to God. There is a God; there is a way to this God; and this way has been made known and made open through the life, death and resurrection of Jesus.

Without in any way losing sight of the fact that Jesus was a human being – who is like us in so many ways – the creeds highlight the fact that there was something fundamentally different about him. Unlike us, he was not a sinner. Tradition-ally, his identity is explored using the 'two natures' framework, which presents Jesus as truly human and truly divine. This often leads Christians to use the pair of titles 'Son of Man' and 'Son of God' to designate the human and divine aspects of Jesus.

The idea that he is the 'Son of God' is not some kind of theological elaboration of the basic New Testament witness. It is already embedded within the New Testament. One of the closing comments made in John's Gospel is particularly important here.

> Now Jesus did many other signs in the presence of his disciples, which are not written in this book. But these are written so that you may come to believe that Jesus is the Messiah, the Son of God, and that through believing you may have life in his name. (John 20.30–31)

John's Gospel presents us with a series of 'signs' – if you like, clues – which point to the full significance of Jesus of Nazareth. We need to look closely at these signs, and ask what they show.

The Gospel accounts of the resurrection of the crucified Jesus are more than a happy ending to a tale of suffering and death. Yes, it is good news that Jesus is restored to those who knew and loved him. But there is far more to the resurrection than this. The resurrection clinches the hints and suggestions seen earlier in the ministry of Jesus, indicating that Jesus had some unique relationship with God.

For Paul, Jesus of Nazareth 'was descended from David according to the flesh and was declared to be Son of God with power according to the spirit of holiness by resurrection from the dead' (Romans 1.3–4). The humanity and divinity of Jesus are like threads woven together in a seamless fabric; they cannot be separated from each other, because they are both an integral part of the pattern.

The New Testament sees the resurrection of Jesus as a public demonstration of his real identity. People may have thought that Jesus of Nazareth was just a lowly Galilean peasant with a gift for teaching and healing. But his resurrection from the dead makes us see him in a very different light.

The Synoptic Gospels (Matthew, Mark and Luke) hint that Jesus enjoyed this status at least from the time of the beginning of his ministry (e.g. Mark 1.11). Some biblical passages even suggest that Jesus possessed this divine status from the beginning of time (John 1.1–14; Philippians 2.6–11; Colossians 1.15–20). At the very least, we may say that the New Testament indicates that there never was a time in his life that Jesus was not already what the resurrection disclosed him to be – the Son of God.

Most of us today find it easiest to start with the assumption that Jesus was a good human being. It's a natural place from which to begin. And it's important to note that neither the New Testament nor the creeds call it into question. They may add to the humanity of Jesus by emphasizing that he did not share our sinfulness, but they do not take away from it. As we read the New Testament, we begin to realize that Jesus is more than human. But at no point does the New Testament suggest that he is less than human.

For some reason, a few early Christian writers, however, seem to have believed that it was dishonourable for Jesus to have been properly human. They argued that he may have had the outward appearance of a man, but in reality he was God, through and through. This doctrine is sometimes known as 'Docetism' (from the Greek word for 'appearance'). After due consideration, it was rejected by the Church. For a start, it did not fit at all with the New Testament witness to Jesus as a human being, like us in so many ways – except that he is not a sinner. 'We do not have a high priest who is unable to sympathize with our weaknesses, but we have one who in every respect has been tested as we are, yet without sin'

(Hebrews 4.15). Furthermore, it makes Jesus a phantom-like figure – a god who puts on a human costume and merely plays the role of a human being but doesn't have any meaningful connection with the rest of us.

I once watched a television debate between some British politicians. One, known to be a multimillionaire, tried very hard to present himself as an ordinary person, who knew exactly what it was like to be short of money and live on a limited budget. The audience wasn't persuaded. They saw a rich man pretending to be poor in order to win their votes, and rumbled him without the slightest difficulty.

But suppose this rich man had given away his fortune. He would no longer have to pretend to be poor; he really would be poor. I'm sure you will immediately perceive the resonance with this New Testament passage: 'You know the generous act of our Lord Jesus Christ, that though he was rich, yet for your sakes he became poor, so that by his poverty you might become rich' (2 Corinthians 8.9). As we try to make sense of the identity of Jesus of Nazareth, we need to hold fast to the insight that – whatever else he was – he was one of us. Or, to put this another way, he *chose* to become one of us. This way of speaking is much closer to the ideas and the language of the New Testament, and is central to the doctrine of the Incarnation, often summarized in the statement 'the word became flesh and lived among us' (John 1.14). But this is to jump ahead in our discussion.

We've established that Jesus is one who teaches with authority; who heals the sick; and who forgives sin. He is someone who seems able to do things that only God is supposed to be able to do, and that only God is allowed to do. Let's now look at another New Testament title for Jesus, which helps us explore this point further – Jesus as Saviour.

Jesus as Saviour

The third title used in the Creeds is that of 'Saviour'. So what does this mean? The New Testament tells us that Jesus saves his people from their sins (Matthew 1.21); that in his name alone is there salvation (Acts 4.12); that he is the 'pioneer of salvation' (Hebrews 2.10). This fundamental belief lies behind one of the earliest symbols of faith used by Christians: a fish. The five letters spelling out this word in Greek (I–CH–TH–U–S) are an acronym of the Greek form of the Christian slogan 'Jesus Christ, Son of God, Saviour'.

I was marking some student essays, with a classical music radio station playing in the background. On the hour, the station broadcast a news bulletin. One item was about a woman who had been kidnapped by bandits, and had now been freed after a gun battle with armed police. One policeman died while setting her free. 'That man was my saviour!' the relieved woman declared.

It was a great soundbite. But it spoke to me deeply. The essay I had been reading was a student's rather inadequate attempt to bring out the full significance of the doctrine of redemption. It was a dull essay, poorly written and lacking sparkle. But my real concern was that the essay treated redemption simply as an abstract idea. My student was hopelessly preoccupied with abstract and impersonal theories about the meaning of the cross. As I listened to the news broadcast, a naughty thought went through my mind. 'That woman knows more about redemption than my theological student!'

Why did I think that? Let me try and explain. It seemed to me that my student was locked into a world of cold logic, fixated on sorting out the consistency of his theology. The rescued woman was trapped, in a hopeless situation from which she could not escape. Her hopes of rescue lay entirely in someone else being willing to take on the bandits, overwhelm them and set her free. It was easy for me to appreciate the hopelessness and helplessness of her situation, and the distress she must have experienced.

Then she was set free. One of her 'saviours' died, so that her joy of liberation was tinged with the deep sadness of his death. But she would remember him for the rest of her life. Without his sacrifice, she might well have remained a hostage – perhaps even a dead hostage. This dramatic rescue was a life-changing event. I wondered what the woman felt like as she was led by her liberators from the darkness of the cave where she had been imprisoned into the bright light of day – and freedom.

Now perhaps I was being unfair to my student. But it seemed to me he had missed so much about the Christian vision of salvation, reducing it to some kind of paper transaction. He seemed to have overlooked the deep personal, existential and emotional richness of the great theme of salvation in Christ, hinted at in one of the great Old Testament prophecies: 'The LORD, your God, is in your midst, a warrior who gives victory; he will rejoice over you with gladness, he will renew you in his love; he will exult over you with loud singing as on a day of festival' (Zephaniah 3.17–18).

Why is this idea of salvation so important? It's all about the hope of transformation. Things don't have to be like this. *We* don't have to be like this. Something can be done to change us – to break the power of death and sin, and to give us hope and meaning. The New Testament is saturated with the belief that the coming of Jesus changes everything. Jesus is the saviour who breaks the power of sin, and heals the deepest wounds of the human soul.

Yet the Old Testament is emphatic that God is the only one who can save. This point is made with special force in some of the great prophetic writings, especially those dating from the time of the exile in Babylon:

> There is no other god besides me, a righteous God and a Saviour; there is no one besides me. Turn to me and be saved, all the ends of the earth! For I am God, and there is no other.
>
> (Isaiah 45.21–22)

Only God can save. But Jesus of Nazareth is our Saviour. So what are we to make of the identity of Jesus? Who must Jesus *be* if he is indeed able to save? As we saw earlier, the resurrection had a decisive influence on Christian thinking about the identity and significance of Jesus. Paul considered that this event demonstrated that Jesus was the Son of God (Romans 1.3–4). However, it's probably fair to say that during Jesus' earthly ministry his true identity was veiled. The clues were certainly there to be seen: Jesus forgave sins – something that only God was meant to do. But nobody seems to have managed to piece together the various bits of the picture. A modern analogy may help us to make sense of this.

The spring of 2013 saw the publication of a crime novel entitled *The Cuckoo's Calling* by Robert Galbraith. Little was known about its first-time author except that he had 'a background in the army and the civilian security industry'. Several reviewers expressed delight at the book, which they felt breathed new life into a somewhat weary literary genre. Yet there were some puzzles. How could an unknown author write such an assured debut novel? And how had he managed to develop such an extensive appreciation of women's fashion?

In July 2013 the mystery was solved, thanks to a security lapse at a firm of copyright lawyers. The book had been written by none other than J. K. Rowling, the celebrity author of the Harry Potter series of novels, who had used a pseudonym so she could explore writing detective fiction without attracting any of the usual hype. The moment her true identity was exposed, sales of the novel rocketed.

Robert Galbraith was J. K. Rowling. There were clues in the text for those sharp enough to spot them, and some had already guessed. But no one could really have known for sure until Rowling herself decided to make her authorship public knowledge, confirming the leaked information.

The resurrection of Jesus of Nazareth confirmed what the hints and clues of the ministry of Jesus suggested – that he was indeed the Son of God. Or to put this another way, God publicly affirmed the true identity of Jesus of Nazareth by raising him from the dead. This theme is prominent in Peter's great sermon on the Day of Pentecost: speaking to a Jewish audience, he declares that the resurrection established and proclaimed the true identity and significance of Jesus of Nazareth. 'God has made him both Lord and Messiah' (Acts 2.36).

As we saw earlier, Peter's use of the title 'Lord' to refer to Jesus of Nazareth is picked up by the creeds. What do the creeds want us to understand when they refer to Jesus as 'our Lord'?

Jesus as Lord

The declaration that 'Jesus is Lord' is found at several points in the New Testament, often in contexts that suggest it was seen as a basic declaration of commitment to the Christian faith (Romans 10.9; 1 Corinthians 12.3). The early Christians didn't really have creeds, and a simple statement like 'Jesus is Lord' would be regarded as a soundbite summary of what they believed.

Let's consider what this title tells us about Jesus of Nazareth. 'Lord' has two main senses in the New Testament. It may be used to indicate respect, as when Martha addresses Jesus in these verses in John's Gospel: 'Martha said to Jesus, "Lord, if you had been here, my brother would not have died. But even now I know that God will give you whatever you ask of him"' (John 11.21–22).

However, there are many other passages in the New Testament where Jesus is referred to as 'the Lord' – for example, 'Everyone who calls on the name of the Lord shall be saved' (Romans 10.13). Similarly, the 'church of God' consists of 'those who in every place call on the name of our Lord Jesus Christ' (1 Corinthians 1.2). The term is here used to acknowledge Jesus's unique relationship to God, and its momentous implications for believers.

It would be helpful at this point to explore how the word 'Lord' was used in the Old Testament. Old Testament writers tended to use a 'cypher' of four letters (often referred to as the Tetragrammaton, from the Greek words for 'four' and 'letters') to represent the sacred name of God, and Greek-speaking Jews often translated this cypher as 'Lord'. (Modern translations of the Old Testament generally print this word 'LORD' in capital letters.)

Let's get technical for a minute. When the Old Testament was translated into Greek, the Greek word *kyrios* ('Lord') was regularly used to translate the sacred name of God from the Hebrew (6,156 out of 6,823 times, to be exact). This Greek word came to be an accepted way of referring directly and specifically to the God of Israel. The historian Josephus tells us that the Jews refused to call the Roman emperor *kyrios*, because they regarded this name as reserved for God alone.

Yet the writers of the New Testament had no hesitation in using 'Lord' to refer to Jesus. These were not ill-informed or muddled people, ignorant of the Jewish background to the name, but writers like Paul who understood perfectly well the implications of using such a term. They regarded the evidence concerning Jesus, especially his resurrection from the dead, as compelling them to speak of him in this way. Let's trace a couple of Old Testament prophecies to illustrate.

The prophet Joel tells of a coming period in the history of the people of God in which the Spirit of God will be poured out upon all people (Joel 2.28). On that day, 'everyone who calls on the name of the LORD shall be saved' (Joel 2.32). This prophecy is referenced in Peter's great sermon on the day of Pentecost (Acts 2.17–21), which ends with the declaration that 'everyone who calls on the name of the Lord shall be saved' (Acts 2.21). But Peter makes it clear that the 'Lord' in question is none other than Jesus of Nazareth, and thus publicly declares the exalted status and identity of the risen Christ.

Another well-known example of this same development is found in Paul's letters. The prophet Isaiah had spoken of a coming day in which all people would worship the Lord God of Israel. 'To me every knee shall bow, every tongue shall swear' (Isaiah 45.23). Paul interprets this prophecy as applying to the risen Jesus:

> Therefore God also highly exalted him and gave him the name
> that is above every name, so that at the name of Jesus every
> knee should bend, in heaven and on earth and under the earth,
> and every tongue should confess that Jesus Christ is Lord, to
> the glory of God the Father.   (Philippians 2.9–11)

In summary, the New Testament writers were of the view
that as God had raised Jesus from the dead, he was to be
regarded as having equal status with God. This meant that
he too was to be worshipped, and we can see clear evidence
of this in the disciples' response to the 'Great Commission'
at the end of Matthew's Gospel: 'When they saw him, they
worshipped him' (Matthew 28.16–20).

Thus far, we've looked at the compacted understanding
of the identity of Jesus of Nazareth set out in the creed's
succinct statement 'I believe in Jesus Christ, [God's] only
Son, our Lord.' But there are other ways of speaking of Jesus
used in the New Testament that can help us grasp something
more of his significance. Let's move on and look at one of
these – the idea of Jesus as a mediator.

Jesus as mediator between God and humanity

Jesus, we are told, is the 'one mediator between God and
humankind' (1 Timothy 2.5). We're all familiar with the idea
of mediation. A stormy personal relationship, an industrial
dispute or an international crisis may all be alleviated by the
diplomacy of a 'go-between', who has a foot in each camp
and so can represent each party faithfully to the other.

Here's a classic scenario from the late Victorian era. A father
and son have a major disagreement about something – it
might be the direction of the family business, the woman
the son wants to marry or the son's political views. Tensions

soar. A massive row takes place in the drawing room after dinner. The father throws his son out of the family home, and threatens to disinherit him.

Who is going to sort things out? The great mediator in so many family melodramas of this period was the mother. She would plead the father's case with the son, and the son's with the father. As the father's wife, and the son's mother, she was uniquely placed to gain their confidence and restore the broken relationship.

Of course, things have changed a lot since the Victorian age. For many of us, mediation is about finding a neutral arbitrator in a dispute. We might get into an argument with our neighbours about their dog barking through the night; with a work colleague we believe isn't doing her job properly; or with a company that fails to deliver an item we ordered. A mediator in any of these instances would be someone both we and the other party are prepared to trust so the dispute may be resolved.

There are, naturally, some important differences between human mediators and Jesus of Nazareth. First, the modern 'arbitrator' is someone who can maintain a neutral position. He won't take sides in the dispute and has no personal interest in it, apart from his desire to get it sorted out. The Victorian analogy of the mother as mediator actually brings us much closer to the Christian understanding of mediation. She is passionately committed to both father and son and wants to reconcile them as an expression of her love. In a not dissimilar way, Jesus, far from being a professional mediator, willingly gives his life to achieve his supreme goal – the reconciliation of God and humanity. Jesus represents God to us, telling us what God is like, explaining that things have gone wrong and that reconciliation is needed, and making it possible for us to renew our broken and damaged relationship with God. That's what Paul is getting at when he declares that 'in Christ God was reconciling the world to himself' (2 Corinthians 5.19).

But there's yet more. Mediation is, after all, a two-way process. To go back to our Victorian family analogy, the mother represents the father to the son – and the son to the father. Jesus of Nazareth mediates God to us – in word, in deed, and in person. But he also mediates us to God. He pleads our case to God. That's one of the points that Paul makes in declaring his faith in 'Christ Jesus, who died, yes, who was raised, who is at the right hand of God, who indeed intercedes for us' (Romans 8.34).

Now there is a lot more that could be said about the rich imagery and vocabulary that the New Testament uses to express its beliefs about the identity and meaning of Jesus of Nazareth. But we need to move on and reflect on a way of thinking about Jesus that the Christian Church has come to see as a 'gold standard' – the best, the most rewarding, the most profound approach to understanding the central figure of the Christian faith. It's time to explore the idea of incarnation.

3

Incarnation: the Word became flesh

———•◦•———

I began my academic career as a scientist, and I still have an active interest in the field. A few years back, I read a biography of J. Robert Oppenheimer (1904–67), one of the twentieth century's most colourful scientists. He was widely regarded during his lifetime as one of America's greatest physicists. But he is now remembered mainly as the 'father of the atomic bomb'. During the Second World War, Oppenheimer played a key role in the Manhattan Project, which led to the development of the atom bomb, and its use against Japan in the summer of 1945.

Two things remained in my mind after reading the biography. One was the moral ambiguity of science. It can be used to do some great things – like heal diseases, and extend human life. And it can also be used to create weapons of mass destruction, intended to obliterate human life. It is an uneasy thought for scientists. But what impressed me above all was a memorable remark Oppenheimer made after the Second World War, as he realized how important it was to meet and talk to people if you wanted to really understand them. 'The best way to send information is to wrap it up in a person.'[1] It's a great quote – and it's right.

Incarnation: God in the flesh

Messages can easily go wrong. I love a story that goes back to the days of telegrams. A couple were getting married. A relative of the bride, unable to attend the ceremony, sent a telegram to be read out at the reception afterwards. To keep the telegram as short (and inexpensive) as possible, he simply referred to a biblical text: 1 John 4.18. It was a very appropriate text. He expected someone to find the text in a Bible and read it aloud to the assembled company at the reception. 'There is no fear in love, but perfect love casts out fear.'

Unfortunately, the telegraph company got the text wrong. They missed out the '1'. So it was not 1 John 4.18 that was finally read out to the astonished guests, but John 4.18. 'You have had five husbands, and the one you have now is not your husband.' The moral is clear! If you want people to understand you, you don't send messages. You go to speak to them yourself.

And that's one of the core themes of the central Christian idea of 'incarnation'. God doesn't send messages. God doesn't even send a messenger. God comes to us, dwells with us, and speaks to us. The letter to the Hebrews is especially helpful on this point. In the Old Testament, God spoke to people in various ways – for example, by sending messengers. Yet this is to be seen as a long process of preparation of human hearts and minds for something still greater – the coming of God himself, in person.

> Long ago God spoke to our ancestors in many and various ways by the prophets, but in these last days he has spoken to us by a Son, whom he appointed heir of all things, through whom he also created the worlds. He is the reflection of God's glory and the exact imprint of God's very being, and he sustains all things by his powerful word. (Hebrews 1.1–3)

It's a theme that is reflected in the powerful theological punches we find in so many Christmas carols. Charles Wesley's great carol 'Hark! the herald angels sing' – which was originally published with the title 'Hark, how all the welkin rings' ('welkin' being an old English word for 'sky' or 'heaven') – has a particularly compelling verse:

> Veiled in flesh the Godhead see:
> Hail, the incarnate Deity!
> Pleased as man with man to dwell,
> Jesus, our Emmanuel!

For Wesley, hymns were an important supplement to the somewhat terse and unappealing statements of the creeds. They could communicate the basics of the Christian faith to ordinary churchgoers, while at the same time providing spiritual nourishment to the theologically educated. Regular singing of these hymns imprinted words and phrases in people's memories and imaginations. Preachers could then unpack the meaning of those words, helping congregations go deeper into their faith (and get more out of singing hymns).

So what does it mean to speak about 'the incarnate Deity', or 'God incarnate'? The word 'incarnate' is derived from the Latin and literally means 'in the flesh'. It expresses the insight of John 1.14: 'the Word became flesh, and lived among us'. Let us unpack this a little. 'The Word' (the term used for one who is living, imperishable, creative and divine) 'became flesh' (the term used for what is creaturely, perishable, finite, mortal and human) 'and lived among us'.

The Christian faith affirms the momentous truth that, in the words of G. K. Chesterton, 'holy things could have a habitation and that divinity need not disdain the limits of time and space.' The stable in which Christ was born is 'a place of dreams come true'. Things that we dared not hope for unfold before our eyes. The great hopes and longings of humanity can be seen, not as delusions, but as intuitions of the deeper structure of reality. Wesley himself caught this sense of expectation in his famous hymn 'Come, thou long-expected Jesus', written in 1744. The hopes of all humanity will find their fulfilment in Jesus, the incarnate God.

> Israel's strength and consolation,
> Hope of all the earth Thou art;
> Dear desire of every nation,
> Joy of every longing heart.

The idea of 'incarnation' means that we are dealing with – and talking about! – a God who chooses to take on frail and mortal human nature, who humbly enters into human history and experiences deprivation and suffering as a human being. Jesus of Nazareth comes to offer us God's unfailing love and abiding presence, not through the exercise of power but through his suffering, death on the cross, and resurrection. The Incarnation is about God breaking down the barriers between earth and heaven. By sharing our life on earth, Jesus – as God incarnate – brings heaven to our lives on earth and invites us to share his life in heaven.

We mustn't think of the Incarnation just as some kind of theological shorthand for the events of Christmas, in which Christians mark the birth of Jesus of Nazareth and celebrate its deeper significance. Or even for the events of Epiphany, which is the main day of rejoicing and present-giving in many Christian countries, since it marks the moment when people first started to take notice of Jesus, sensing his glory and beginning to glimpse who he really is.[2]

The doctrine of Incarnation may indeed focus on the birth of Jesus, but it is not limited to it. In speaking about 'God incarnate', we are not simply affirming that God chose to enter history in Bethlehem. We recognize that 'incarnation' extends to embrace the person that the infant Jesus became, above all the crucified Saviour, and the risen and ascended Christ. That's what the Nicene Creed is getting at in its clear and concise statement: 'For us and for our salvation he came down from heaven, and was incarnate of the Holy Spirit.' God's entry into history begins the great story of salvation, which reaches its climax in the cross and resurrection of Jesus of Nazareth.

Why Christians believe in the Incarnation

Earlier we noted how the creeds are an invitation to discover aspects of our faith which we imperfectly understand, or perhaps fear are fundamentally irrational. For some, the doctrine of the Incarnation could come into one – or both – of these categories. Like the doctrine of the Trinity, it seems to be a blot of foolishness on the landscape of a perfectly reasonable faith. Couldn't we do without it and keep things simple?

Dorothy L. Sayers, one of the greatest lay theologians of the twentieth century, had an answer for those who doubted the relevance of the Incarnation. It was there because it needed to be. 'Dogmas are not a set of arbitrary regulations invented a priori by a committee of theologians enjoying a bout of all-in dialectical wrestling.' Rather they defended vital insights which, if lost, would condemn the Church to irrelevance. The central dogma of the Incarnation is what keeps Christianity Christian. 'If Christ was only a man, then he is entirely irrelevant to any thought about God; if he is only God, then he is entirely irrelevant to any experience of human life.'[3]

Sayers brings out the point that Christianity is shaped by a theological logic that leads inexorably to the doctrine of the Trinity on the one hand, and the doctrine of the Incarnation on the other. This doesn't make either of these doctrines any easier to understand. But it does help us appreciate that neither is some kind of optional extra, like our choice of topping on an ice cream. They are woven into the fabric of the Christian faith.

In part, our problem comes from the ideas we've absorbed from our cultural context. You can't live in the West without being influenced by its assumptions. These have been shaped by the rationalist culture of the eighteenth century – above all, its belief that reality could be reduced to something that reason could master. As a result, God and Jesus have come to be trapped within rationalist cages, like majestic tigers imprisoned, and unable to show themselves for what they really are. The stereotypes of Christ as a 'good religious teacher' or 'a prophetic voice' reflect this development. They help us avoid intellectual discomfort by simply ignoring the bits that don't fit this rationalist template.

That's precisely what the creeds – especially the Nicene Creed – want to prevent us doing. They don't give us the option of holding on to our preconceived ideas about what Jesus ought to be like. As Dorothy Sayers saw so clearly, no existing mould or template is good enough to do justice to the full significance of Jesus. The Church had to invent one specially for this purpose.

Now, of course, Jesus of Nazareth really was a teacher and a prophet, and there is nothing wrong in affirming that.

The trouble comes when we try to limit him to just one of those categories and lose sight of the fact that there may be many more aspects to explore, and to weave into our thinking about Jesus.

With my background in the natural sciences, I try to keep up my reading in the field – especially in the fascinating world of the history and philosophy of science. I find it offers a liberating alternative to the simplistic understandings of science held by some recent atheist writers – such as Richard Dawkins's insistence that science proves all its beliefs. As we saw in *Faith and the Creeds*, it doesn't, and the reason it doesn't is that it can't! Now there's a particular aspect of the philosophy of science which helps us when we think about the identity of Jesus of Nazareth: it's the approach called 'critical realism'.

The basic idea of critical realism is that reality has many levels and that in order to see things in full, all these levels need to be taken into account. Many scientists would argue that science is about looking for the 'big picture' – the one that makes most sense of experimental observations. Whether we're considering the origins of the universe or the movement of the planets, the best theory is always going to be the one that weaves together the greatest number of threads, or fits the greatest number of snapshots into the panorama.

Sir Arthur Conan Doyle's fictional detective Sherlock Holmes was noted for his passionate search for an explanation that made sense of all the clues. In the same way, Christians try to assemble the various snapshots of Jesus – such as Jesus as healer, as teacher and as Saviour – in the way that best holds all these together (as mentioned in Chapter 1). What is the 'big picture' that makes most sense of all the clues? That tells the truth, and the *whole* truth?

Let's think about this a little more. I love detective novels. I spent two years studying at Cambridge University, and would often go to the open-air market in the centre of town to see what the booksellers had to offer me. At that stage, I was a great fan of the detective novels of Erle Stanley Gardner, featuring his greatest creation, the lawyer Perry Mason. Although I had copies of most of his novels by that time, every now and then one would turn up that I hadn't read. I remember how excited I was when I not only found a book that I had not yet read – I think it was *The Case of the Moth-Eaten Mink* – but it was very cheap. I bought it, and went back to my room to begin reading it.

It was one of his best, and I soon got into the plot. As the suspense built up, I became more and more engaged with the clues that Mason had discovered, and wondered how he would weave them together in an exciting courtroom climax. As I turned over a page, I realized to my horror that the last thirty pages were missing. That was why it was so cheap!

A good detective novel grabs the reader's attention as the detective searches for the murderer. We are set alongside the fictional detective, as he or she discovers clues, and gradually builds up a picture of what must have happened, in order to uncover the identity of the murderer in an exciting climax. It is only at this point that we readers find out whether we have noticed all the clues, and worked out their real significance.

But whereas detective novels are basically 'whodunnits', the Gospels are best seen as 'whowasits'. They are interested in establishing the identity and significance of their central figure, rather than with picking out a murderer from a number of possible suspects. The Gospel writers allow us to see and hear what the disciples heard, and force us to ask much the same questions that they must have asked before us. What do these things mean? Just who is this man? And just as the writers of detective novels single out, or draw our attention to, significant things (in other words, clues) which we might otherwise have overlooked, so the Gospel writers do the same.

It is so easy to overlook clues. Something may take place which appears to be insignificant at the time, and yet assumes a much greater significance later, as its full meaning becomes obvious. A good example is Conan Doyle's story 'Silver Blaze', which tells of how the great fictional detective Sherlock Holmes investigates an attack on a valuable racehorse. One important clue is that the watchdog did not bark during the night of the attack. This fact is observed, but its significance is only grasped later, when Holmes points out that it could only mean that the dog knew the intruder.

Something similar can be seen in the Gospels, where the fact that something did not happen is often important. For example, Mark notes that Jesus was silent before his accusers at his trial (Mark 14.61), where he might have been expected to defend himself. The significance of this silence can be seen in the light of the silence of the suffering servant (Isaiah 53.7) before his accusers. This mysterious individual, who features prominently in the prophecy of Isaiah, is widely seen as a redeemer, bearing other people's wounds and sins. Mark wants us to notice this clue, and draw us on to note other parallels between Jesus and this mysterious Old Testament figure.

So how were these clues to be understood? What was really going on? And what do they tell us about the true identity of Jesus of Nazareth? Now, when you're looking for a tool for a job, you have two options. You can start from scratch and invent something that has never been used before, developing it with the needs of the task specifically in mind. The easier option, though, is to take something that's already in use and hope it can be adapted for the new job.

As the first Christians struggled to find the best way of making sense of Jesus,[4] they adopted ideas that were already in use. Some suggested he was like a wandering sage – a dispenser of wisdom – though this limited Jesus's significance to his teaching. Others argued he was like a prophet – a person with an especially close relationship with God. This framework was familiar to many early Christians, and certainly accommodated some of the snapshots of Jesus of Nazareth. For example, there were parallels between Jesus' teaching and healing ministries and those of the prophet Elijah. But events like the resurrection simply didn't fit in at all.

In the end, Christian theologians realized that they couldn't borrow models from Judaism or secular Greek culture. Yes, Jesus was a teacher; yes, Jesus was a prophet – but he was so much more than this. He was also a saviour. And a friend of sinners. And lots of other things as well. No existing way of thinking about the expected Messiah did justice to the true identity of Jesus of Nazareth. The old wineskins just couldn't cope with this new wine (Mark 2.22).

And so the doctrine of the Incarnation was developed, not as a result of church politics or pressure from the Roman emperor Constantine, but simply because the weight of evidence demanded this verdict. The doctrine of the Incarnation provided the best 'big picture' that made sense of all the little pictures – such as Jesus as a teacher, or a healer. Each of these snapshots would turn out to be an essential part of the panorama of incarnation, but none was sufficient on its own.

Some suggest that the doctrine of the Incarnation isn't really biblical. After all, they rightly point out, the word 'incarnation' is never used in the New Testament. The technical term may not be there, but the idea certainly is. Many New Testament scholars would argue that the idea of 'incarnation' is just a rephrasing of the core insight of John 1.14: 'And the Word became flesh and lived among us.' The doctrine of the Incarnation is what we get when we join up the dots – when we grasp the 'big picture' that underlies the New Testament's rich witness to the identity of Jesus of Nazareth. All the pieces of the jigsaw are there for us to put together, allowing us to see the pattern that results.

Jesus of Nazareth: the big picture

One of the most obvious differences between the Nicene Creed and the Apostles' Creed is the terms they use in talking about Jesus. The Apostles' Creed sets out the basic framework of the story of Jesus, using titles such as 'Son of God' and 'Saviour'. The Nicene Creed employs a much more developed vocabulary. It affirms that Jesus of Nazareth is 'true God from true God', 'of one Being with the Father', and 'was incarnate of the Holy Spirit and the Virgin Mary'. So why this striking difference?

The answer lies in the historical origins of the Nicene Creed. As we saw in *Faith and the Creeds*, the Council of Nicaea was summoned by the Roman emperor Constantine in 325. Constantine, who had recently converted to Christianity, declared that Christianity was now a legal religion, and called a gathering of Christian bishops to hammer out an agreed summary of their faith. They met in the town of Nicaea in Asia Minor (now Iznik, in modern Turkey).

Constantine's reasons for convening this council of bishops were complex, but one of his major concerns was to secure unity within the Christian churches. Christianity was becoming the most important religious movement within the Roman Empire, and Constantine was concerned that disagreements within the Church could threaten the unity of the empire. Towards the end of the previous century a highly divisive debate, concerning how Christians should think about Jesus of Nazareth, had split the Church. Not surprisingly, Constantine wanted things sorted out. He had no intention of imposing his own solution. He just wanted Christians to agree among themselves, so that a consensus could be reached. And it was.

The Apostles' Creed offers a positive statement of basic Christian beliefs, a summary of what Christians ought to think. The Nicene Creed is more expansive, and warns us off certain ways of thinking that are inadequate or downright misleading understandings of core Christian beliefs – such as the identity of Jesus of Nazareth. The Nicene Creed lays down some ground rules for thinking about Jesus of Nazareth. Certain ways of understanding him were declared to be inadequate, others were seen as orthodox.

If we think of the range of possible interpretations of Christ's identity and significance as being like a field, the council simply placed a hedge around the good pastureland. It marked off and preserved the area of reliable interpretations of Jesus of Nazareth, and invited us to explore them. Other ways of thinking about him were declared to be inadequate, impoverished or misleading. These are what we would now call 'heresies'.[5]

Heresies often gained popularity because they seemed easy to believe or because they resonated with the cultural values of the age. One that gained support in the third century was known as 'Arianism' after Arius, a popular preacher in the city of Alexandria. It is not entirely clear what led him to develop his way of thinking about Jesus; however, it seems that one of Arius's concerns about the doctrine of the Incarnation was that it caused offence to Greek philosophers, who considered it illogical. Just how could someone be both God and a human being?

Arius came up with an approach that he thought avoided this problem.[6] While acclaiming Jesus as the greatest of God's creatures, surpassing every other aspect of God's creation, Arius insisted that Jesus was not divine in any sense of the term. He was 'first among the creatures' but still part of the created order.

This view was much easier for Arius to reconcile with the ideas of God preferred by Greek philosophers; his critics, however, argued that the very few advantages of the theory were totally eclipsed by its drawbacks. Athanasius of Alexandria, who is often singled out as one of the early Church's most important theologians, had no doubt what the problems with Arianism were.

First, he argued, it represented a serious distortion of the witness to Jesus of Nazareth in the New Testament. Arius argued that certain passages which spoke of Jesus in highly exalted terms had to be seen as polite or respectful exaggerations of his significance. Athanasius countered that they were to be taken seriously and given due weight. He had little difficulty in pointing to some of the texts that were stumbling blocks for Arius. What about the confession of 'Doubting Thomas' on seeing the risen Christ: 'My Lord and my God!' (John 20.28)? Arius insisted that Jesus was a genuine human being; Athanasius believed this was only part of the story.

Second, Athanasius pointed to the practice of worshipping Jesus which, as we have seen, was already taking place within the New Testament, and was a regular aspect of Christian worship in the second century and beyond.[7] Was this an expression of respect, an indication of personal allegiance? Or was it something much deeper that reflected an awareness of Jesus' true identity as God incarnate? Athanasius argued that the overall patterns of devotion evident in the New Testament fitted easily and naturally into the view that Jesus of Nazareth was truly human and truly divine.

Third, Athanasius noted that both the New Testament and the Christian tradition speak of Jesus of Nazareth doing things which only God can do, including judging us. He echoed the views of earlier Christian theologians, such as Clement of Rome: 'We must therefore think about Jesus Christ as about God, as the judge of the living and the dead.'[8] Athanasius was particularly anxious to emphasize that the New Testament portrays Jesus of Nazareth as the saviour of humanity. Only God can save, so if Jesus is, as Arius suggested, merely a particularly gifted or prestigious human being, he cannot be our saviour. And if Jesus is not our saviour, he is part of the problem, not a solution to the problem.

Athanasius took this point further. If Jesus is just another human being, no matter how exalted, in what way is he qualified to speak about God? How can he show us what God is like? Once more, Athanasius pointed to the rich witness of the New Testament and drew out its theological consequences. If Jesus is a human being, like us, then the quality of his knowledge of God is on the same level as ours. He can only speak to us about God from a human standpoint, no matter how enlightened.

But if Jesus is God – as the doctrine of the Incarnation affirms – everything changes. First, Jesus can show and teach us what God is like – because he is God. He can make promises on God's behalf. To put it simply, the divinity of Christ establishes a firm and unassailable theological link between God and Jesus. One of Scotland's greatest theologians, Hugh Ross Mackintosh (1870–1936), used to hammer home this point in his theological lectures at New College, Edinburgh, where he was Professor of Divinity for over 30 years: 'When I look into the face of Jesus Christ and see the face of God, I know that I have not seen that face elsewhere and could not see it else-how, for he and the Father are one.'[9]

Jesus is both a lens that allows us to see God clearly, and a gateway that gives us access to the presence of God and insight into our own situation. As G. K. Chesterton once remarked, Christianity provides us with 'that longest and strangest telescope – the telescope through which we could see the star upon which we dwelt'.

The two natures of Jesus

The classic Christian understanding of Jesus is often summed up in the phrase 'two natures'. Like all theological slogans, this can sound a little too neat and slick, but it puts into words, however inadequately, the distilled essence of Christian reflection on the identity and significance of Jesus: he is truly human and truly divine.

In speaking about Jesus of Nazareth like this, Christians do not mean that the Incarnation is about God 'becoming' human in the sense that God stopped being God and started being a human instead. The Incarnation is not about God ceasing to be God, but about God additionally taking up human nature. To put this another way, Jesus of Nazareth was not God minus some elements of divinity, but God plus everything that resulted from God assuming a human nature, and entering into human history. The Incarnation is about an enriched, not a diluted, vision of God.

Nor do Christians think that the doctrine of the Incarnation means that God ceased to be in heaven, and became exclusively and totally located in Jesus of Nazareth. The New Testament is clear that God did not relocate to earth. John Calvin (1509–64) is one of many theologians who tried to put this difficult idea into words.

> While the Word in his immeasurable essence was united with human nature in one person, we do not imagine that he was limited as a result. Here is something marvellous: the Son of God descended from heaven in such a way that, without leaving heaven, he willed to be born in the virgin's womb, to go about on earth, and to hang upon the cross.[10]

It's not an easy idea to grasp. Let me share an approach which helps me make sense of this. I can still remember the sense of excitement that I and countless others experienced when Apollo 11 landed on the moon in July 1969. I stayed up very late to watch the live broadcast of Neil Armstrong becoming the first human being to set foot on the moon, and heard his words: 'That's one small step for man, one giant leap for mankind.' The Apollo 11 team brought about 20 kilograms of moonrock back to earth with them, so that scientists could study samples of the moon for the very first time.

I often think about that event when reflecting on the Incarnation. The moon is still there in the sky. But we now have an authentic sample of moonrock on earth. Sure, it's an inadequate analogy. But it helps us grasp one point. The moon remains where it is. But in 1969, we were able to hold part of the moon in our hands, touching it for the first time. As Germanus of Constantinople put it in an eighth-century hymn still sung to this day, 'The Word becomes incarnate and yet remains on high.'

So far, so good. But the Nicene Creed uses more technical language to refer to Jesus of Nazareth. Jesus, it declares, is 'true God from true God' and 'of one Being with the Father'. So why does it use these phrases? And what are we to make of them?

Let's begin with the first of these. Why the emphasis on Jesus being 'true God from true God'? The basic idea is simple: we can trust Jesus to show and tell us what God is like. Jesus of Nazareth is the incarnation of the God of Christianity – the one true God who created the world before entering into it in order to redeem it. Those who want to know what God is like need only look to the face of Jesus. 'Whoever has seen me has seen the Father,' he states (John 14.9). To put this in a dangerously simple way: Jesus is able to tell us about God and show us what God is like precisely because he is God. He is the lens through which we see God most reliably.

We all know people who are hypocritical – the colleague at work who praises the boss to his face and rubbishes him behind his back; or the friend who supports us when we make a difficult decision then tells other people how foolish she thinks we're being. The problem with being 'two-faced' is not that a person is operating in two different environments or contexts. It's that the 'face' being presented is totally different in each case – almost as if someone were two distinct people. The New Testament, however, portrays Jesus of Nazareth as a single person, rooted both in the reality of

God and in the reality of human nature. Jesus faces two ways, but the 'face' presented is one and the same. He really does show us the face of God.

But what of the second statement? What does it mean to say that Jesus is 'of one Being with the Father'? Here we need to spend a few moments in the technical world of Greek philosophy. The word translated as 'Being' (or, in a number of translations of the creed, 'substance') really means something like 'essential nature' or 'inward identity'. As we noted earlier, the Nicene Creed resolved a debate within the Church over the best way of expressing the identity of Jesus of Nazareth. One option was to suggest that Jesus is like God; the other was to say that Jesus really is God. The Nicene Creed made its views clear: the best way of understanding Jesus is to affirm that he is the full embodiment of God.

The council had no time for the idea that a busy and overworked God might decide to send a deputy or delegate to be responsible for running the universe and saving the human race. Following precedents in classical Greek thought, such a 'deputy' could be thought of as a subordinate figure – some kind of divinity who wasn't quite on the same level as God. But this does not fit at all well with the witness to Jesus of Nazareth in the New Testament, where Jesus is clearly thought of as coming, not merely to bring us some kind of communication from God, but to enable us to have fellowship with God – and to show us what that life of fellowship with God looked like in practice. Jesus of Nazareth is thus both the foundation and an illustration of the redeemed life.

Let's now consider the significance of the Incarnation in more detail.

The significance of the Incarnation

Which God lies at the heart of the Christian faith? The New Testament answer is clear: 'the God and Father of our Lord Jesus Christ' (Ephesians 1.3). Christians believe and trust in the God of Jesus of Nazareth, that is, we believe in the same God as Jesus. The German theologian Jürgen Moltmann (b. 1926) found himself drawn to Jesus as he read the Gospel narratives. He began his pilgrimage of faith by believing in God as a mark of respect for Jesus. But as he reflected on the New Testament, he began to realize that there was a more complex relationship involved. Later in his career, he framed his approach in a slightly different way but one that remains helpful. 'Christians believe in Jesus for God's sake, and in God for Jesus's sake'.[11] What Moltmann is getting at is summed up beautifully in the 'farewell discourses' of John's Gospel. 'Do not let your hearts be troubled. Believe in God, believe also in me' (John 14.1). To trust God is to trust Jesus.

Let's explore this a little further. If we are to trust God, we must have trustworthy knowledge of God, and Jesus is not only the best image we have of God: he is an image of God that is authorized by God. We are meant to focus on Jesus of Nazareth – his life, death and resurrection – in reflecting on who God is, and what God is like. Jesus is the 'image of the invisible God' (Colossians 1.15), the 'reflection of God's glory and the exact imprint of God's very being' (Hebrews 1.3). The Christian idea of the Incarnation brings out this fundamental aspect of the identity of Jesus: he is the one who shows us and tells us what God is really like. To trust in God is thus also to trust in the one who makes God known.

Here's a story that might make the idea of Jesus as 'the image of God' easier to grasp. Back in 1976, a colleague and I spent time travelling in Turkey and Iran. Border controls were much more relaxed in those days, and as I was waiting to present my passport at the desk, the person immediately in front of me got involved in an argument with the Iranian immigration official. His passport photo did not match his face. 'You can't trust cameras!' the traveller protested. 'It's a bad picture. I don't really look like that!' And he gestured furiously at his passport photo. After a few moments staring at the photograph, the official shrugged his shoulders, stamped the passport and waved him through.

None of us wants to look like our passport photo. Sure, it's an image of us. But it can be a bad and misleading image, bearing little relation to what we really look like. Remember Henry VIII and Anne of Cleves? Anne's German family connections led Henry to think she might be worth marrying to secure an alliance between England and Germany. However, he had never met Anne, and had no idea what she looked like. As photography had not yet been invented, the artist Hans Holbein was commissioned to paint her portrait. Henry liked what he saw, and the marriage contract was duly arranged. When Henry met Anne for the first time, his courtiers reported that he did not like her looks. Holbein's portrait was too flattering! In the end, the marriage was cancelled, although the two remained friends for the rest of Henry's life.

Pictures matter in everyday life, and they matter just as much in the life of faith. The doctrine of the Incarnation reassures us that Jesus of Nazareth is the most trustworthy picture of God we possess. We simply do not have access to any better image than this. To trust in the Christian God is to trust the means by which we know this God – supremely, through the words and deeds of Jesus of Nazareth. He is the point of intersection between God and ourselves, the window through which we see God, and the highway by which we come to God. Jesus does not simply tell us about God; he shows us God. Jesus does not simply point out the way to God; he takes us to God. The Incarnation is all about bringing God to us, and us to God. That's why the image of Jesus of Nazareth as mediator, which we looked at in the previous chapter, is so helpful.

Let's now look at a classic statement of the doctrine of the Incarnation, found in the writings of the great theologian Athanasius of Alexandria. In his masterpiece *On the Incarnation of the Word of God*, written around 365, Athanasius set out its basic themes like this:

> So the Son of God became the Son of Man, so that the sons of man, that is, of Adam, might become sons of God. The Word begotten of the Father from on high, inexpressibly, inexplicably, incomprehensibly and eternally, is the one who is born in time here below, of the Virgin Mary, the Mother of God, so that those who are born here in the first place might have a second birth from on high, that is, of God.[12]

The language is dense, but the basic idea is clear. God became incarnate – that is, God entered into human history as a real human being – in order to allow those born in time to be reborn eternally. God became incarnate, so that we might become the children of God. The doctrine of the Incarnation frames and safeguards one of the most dramatic insights of the Christian faith – namely, that the God who created the heavens and the earth chose to come and dwell among us human beings as one of us.

One of my recent research projects involved looking at the correspondence between a group of American pastors and their counterparts in England during the early seventeenth century. The letters had to be transported by sailing ships across the Atlantic Ocean. It was a long and dangerous journey and the letters often took months to arrive. Sometimes the ships never made it across the ocean at all. Yet today, I can send a message to an American colleague in seconds. I've got so used to this that I have lost any sense of amazement over being able to communicate so quickly.

Similarly, as Christians we can become so familiar with the idea of the Incarnation that we lose sight of its wonder. Paul's astonishment and delight at the idea of God humbly entering into history in the form of a servant is evident from his letters – especially the famous 'Christ-hymn' of his letter to the Philippians:

> Though [Jesus of Nazareth] was in the form of God, [he] did not regard equality with God as something to be exploited, but emptied himself, taking the form of a slave, being born in human likeness. And being found in human form, he humbled himself and became obedient to the point of death – even death on a cross. (Philippians 2.6–8)

Paul clearly regards the idea of the sovereign and creator Lord choosing to enter the world in such a humble manner as too wonderful to capture properly in words. Not only does the creator of the world stoop down to enter our history: God enters the world as its servant, and is put to death by the most inhuman form of execution that human ingenuity could devise. The creator and redeemer of humanity willingly suffers the fate that civilized humanity reserved for its worst criminals. God did not send a deputy or representative into the world to bring us to our senses and redeem us. The Father himself set out into the 'far country' to call his lost and wayward children home, so that they might live for ever with him.

C. S. Lewis on the Incarnation

As we have seen, Christmas marks the birth of Jesus of Nazareth, the central figure of the Christian faith. But some readers may still wonder whether there is a disconnection between the singular life of Jesus of Nazareth and the universal relevance of God. What has someone who lived long, long ago got to do with us today? Or with God?

That was the question that troubled C. S. Lewis in 1931. After a period as an atheist, Lewis had recently returned to belief in God. God, he concluded, offered a way of making sense of the world and of human experience, which appealed to both his reason and imagination. But Jesus of Nazareth did not seem to fit into this scheme of things. He seemed superfluous. Why did belief in God have anything to do with him? As he wrote to his close friend Arthur Greeves, he could not see 'how the life and death of Someone Else (whoever he was) 2000 years ago could help us here and now'.[13] How on earth could the life of someone who lived two thousand years ago impact on us now? It's a question that many asked before Lewis, and one that many continue to ask today.

Lewis's answer remains important. After a long conversation with his colleague J. R. R. Tolkien in September 1931, Lewis began to realize that Christianity was not primarily a set of ideas about God and the world. It was about a story – a 'grand narrative', which both captured the imagination and opened up new ways of thinking. The creeds arose from reflection on this true and trustworthy story, which centred and focused on Jesus of Nazareth. When rightly understood, the imaginatively compelling story of the birth of Jesus of Nazareth was about God entering the world, in order to redeem it. The Christmas liturgy and carols set out a powerful vision of a God who enters the world in humility, which is embraced by the imagination as much as it is analysed by reason. We would do well to reflect on Lewis's emphasis on the 'imaginative embrace' of faith. The theme of the Incarnation is impoverished if it is reduced to a mere piece of cold and clinical theological logic.

Lewis explored the theme of incarnation in a highly imaginative way in a remarkable sermon preached in a London church during the Second World War. Lewis had learned how to dive in 1930. Although he initially saw this simply as an enjoyable and exhilarating experience, Lewis began to realize its potential as an analogy for what he was coming to see as a core theme of the Christian faith – the Incarnation. In his sermon, Lewis invited his audience to imagine a diver, who wants to rescue something precious that has fallen into the mud at the bottom of a deep lake. He asks us to imagine the diver plunging

> down through the green and warm and sunlit water into the pitch black, cold, freezing water, down into the mud and slime, then up again, his lungs almost bursting, back again to the green and warm and sunlit water, and then at last out into the sunshine, holding in his hand the dripping thing he went down to get.[14]

And just what is this thing that merited all that effort and risk? It is us, God's wayward creatures! God 'descended into his own universe, and rose again, bringing human nature up with him'.

For Lewis, the doctrine of the Incarnation tells us that God plunged into our world to perform a rescue operation. It can be summed up in the biblical affirmation that the 'Word became flesh and lived among us' (John 1.14). The Greek word translated here as 'lived' more accurately means 'pitched his tent'. It presents us with a powerful image of Israel as a wandering people in the period looked back to by the prophets as a time when she was close to God. As the Israelites travel on the journey of faith, they find a new tent pitched in their midst. God himself has come to dwell among them. And God is with us, as our constant companion and consoler.

The doctrine of the Incarnation solidifies one of the great truths of the Christian faith – that God truly cares for us, not as a passive distant observer, but as an active fellow traveller on the road of human life. If life is a journey, God is our constant companion on that journey. And let's remember where that word 'companion' comes from – a Latin root meaning 'someone that you break bread with' or 'someone who shares your bread'. It's hard not to see the connections with the story of the Road to Emmaus.

This is a theme which the Christian Church recalls every year at Christmas, as it rejoices in the knowledge that its Saviour has not dismissed us as insignificant or devoid of value. So much did our creator and redeemer love us that he chose to enter into his creation in the most lowly manner. One of the finest and best-known statements of this theme is found in Cecil F. Alexander's Christmas carol 'Once in royal David's city':

> He came down to earth from heaven,
> Who is God and Lord of all,
> And his shelter was a stable,
> And his cradle was a stall;
> With the poor, and mean, and lowly,
> Lived on earth our Saviour holy.

We do not have to climb a ladder into heaven in order to find and embrace God. God has come down that ladder in order to meet us where we are, and to embrace us. Our Saviour has come into our home in order to bring us to his home, where we may rest and feast with him. He abides with us, sharing our shame and pain, while making it possible for us to rise above this and one day join him in the halls of the New Jerusalem.

The Incarnation and the journey of faith

We have been opening a series of windows into the Incarnation in the present chapter. Let's now consider how three of the insights we've gained may help us make sense of our faith and cope with our personal journey

First, the Incarnation allows us to picture God. To know Christ is to know God. To have seen Christ is to have seen God. 'Whoever has seen me has seen the Father' (John 14.9). To appreciate the importance of this, let's think about what the love of God is like. We could say that it is infinite, boundless and beyond human telling. But that's not much use. That's saying what the love of God is not like. How can we speak of the love of God for us in a way that appeals to our imaginations, and enables us to picture it in action rather than as an abstract idea?

The doctrine of the Incarnation tells us that the love of God is like the love of someone who willingly lays down his life for his friends (John 15.13). This moving and poignant image drawn from human experience heightens our awareness of the wonder of what God has done for us. We can visualize the love of God as we picture Jesus Christ trudging to Calvary. He did not need to do this; he chose to do it – and he chose to do it for us. What Jesus says tells us what God is like; what Jesus did shows us what God is like.

Second, the Incarnation is about bringing our own stories into contact with the story of God. This idea may seem difficult to grasp, but it is worth taking trouble over. Each of us has our own, unique story, which nobody else shares. But bringing our story into connection with a 'grand narrative' gives it a new significance. It helps us realize our story is part of a greater one, and in one sense, faith is about embracing this 'bigger story' and allowing our own story to contribute to it.

We see this in the Chronicles of Narnia, where C. S. Lewis deftly shows how the children – particularly Lucy Pevensie, who is in many ways the central human character of the series – have their individual stories shaped by the story of the magnificent and noble lion Aslan. Lucy's love for Aslan is expressed in her commitment to him. She wants to do what he wants; she wants to become part of his story.

Lewis thus develops a New Testament theme which has a long history of exploration within the Christian faith. Faith involves putting to death the old self (Galatians 2.20) and rising to a new life. We do not lose our individuality; rather, we gain a new identity, while remaining individuals who are loved by God. As Lewis makes clear in the Chronicles of Narnia, our own stories can become a prison. We can get locked into ways of thinking and acting that are purely self-serving.

Lucy and the other children realize that there is indeed a 'bigger story', and long to become part of it. Yet they are not gatecrashing someone else's story; they were *made* and were *meant* to be part of it. So they surrender their self-centred stories, and replace them with Aslan-centred stories, which give them purpose, value and meaning. That's what the Incarnation affirms – that God enters our history, so we can redirect our own stories to be part of the greater story of God's loving process of putting the world to rights. We have a part to play in that story, and faith is partly about finding, accepting and embracing our God-given roles.

There are many examples of this from which we can learn. Ira Sankey (1840–1908) was a fine singer, who was impressed by Dwight Moody, the greatest revivalist preacher of the second half of the nineteenth century. The two met in Indianapolis in 1870. The next day, Moody asked Sankey to meet him at a street corner. When Sankey arrived, Moody produced a soap-box, and invited Sankey to mount it and sing a hymn. Sankey – who had a magnificent voice – did so. A crowd gathered to hear him. When Sankey had finished, Moody got on the box and delivered a short sermon. Sankey's singing drew many to hear Moody preach. As Sankey developed his ministry, he became one of the greatest writers and arrangers of hymns of his generation. His musical gift was put to new use. Sankey had become part of a greater story.

Third, the Incarnation assures us that God is with us – even in the darkest moments of life. This great theme of the doctrine of the Incarnation is summed up in the name given to Christ at his birth: 'Emmanuel' – 'God is with us' (Matthew 1.20–23). But what exactly does 'God being with us' mean?

Well, first it brings home to us that God is rooting for us. 'If God is for us, who is against us?' (Romans 8.31–32). 'God is with us' thus means that 'God is on our side'.

In the birth of the long-promised Saviour, in his death on the cross of Calvary, and in his resurrection from the dead we have a demonstration, a proof, a guarantee, that God stands by us. When Christians celebrate the Incarnation every Christmas, they are affirming that the God we are dealing with, the God and Father of our Lord Jesus Christ, is not a God who is indifferent to our fate. This God is passionately committed to our salvation, to redeeming us from sin, and to raising us to eternal life on the last day.

'God is with us' thus secondly means that we are dealing with a God who has entered into our human situation, who became a human being and dwelt among us as one of us – someone who knows at first hand what it is like to be frail, mortal and human, to suffer and to die. This is an important point for us to hold on to when we have to face suffering. Jesus has been there before us. God incarnate knows what it is like to experience anguish.

At times, we feel immensely lonely as we journey through life. We often long for companionship on that long and difficult road, especially when it appears dark and dangerous. The doctrine of the Incarnation assures us that the God who has called us to be with him has already travelled that road. The creator has entered the creation, and knows precisely the circumstances we face. Christ has shed tears on the road of human sorrow and suffering before us. God our shepherd journeys with us, even when we walk through the valley of the shadow of death (Psalm 23). We are not alone.

Finally, Jesus does not merely show us what God is like, important though that is; he also gives us a glimpse of what we could be. We shall explore this theme further in the final chapter of this book, as we consider how Jesus of Nazareth helps us shape and live the Christian life.

We now need to turn our attention to the full significance of what Jesus achieved and secured through his death and resurrection. In the next chapter, we will explore what are often referred to as 'theories of the atonement'.

4

Atonement: putting things right

The ancient chapel of King's College, Cambridge is renowned for its annual candlelit Festival of Nine Lessons and Carols. On Christmas Eve, some 1,800 people crowd in for the 3 p.m. service, which is broadcast to millions of listeners around the world.

One of the centrepieces of the chapel is a large seventeenth-century painting by Sir Peter Paul Rubens depicting the Adoration of the Magi – the visit of the mysterious wise men from the east to the infant Jesus. In 1974, the painting was vandalized by intruders. Large crowds gathered to look with sadness at the damaged masterwork. Yet soon afterwards, one visitor recalled, a notice appeared which read 'It is believed this masterpiece can be restored'.

Restoration is a central theme of the Christian doctrine of atonement and an idea that's hardwired into the New Testament. God's masterpiece, the height of creation, has been wounded and damaged. It has fallen and been broken. Yet although we are broken, we can be mended. Our wounds can be healed. Jesus 'himself bore our sins in his body on the cross, so that, free from sins, we might live for righteousness; by his wounds you have been healed' (1 Peter 2.24). We shall be exploring this great theme in more detail in this chapter.

But before we do so, let's look at how Christian thinking about the atonement fits into the bigger scheme of things. Christian theology aims to help us appreciate and understand the 'big picture' of faith in all its fullness. It helps us grasp its comprehensiveness, its richness, and its capacity to make sense of things and offer hope and transformation. The creeds tell us about a glorious, loving and righteous God, who creates a world that goes wrong, and then acts graciously and wondrously in order to renew and redirect it, before finally bringing it to its fulfilment.

Yet it is all too easy to form the impression that Christian doctrines are like watertight compartments, each of which can be studied in isolation from others. It's a neat idea, and may be helpful pedagogically in instructing people in the basics of faith. But it's misleading. Christian beliefs are not a set of individual, unrelated ideas. They are interconnected, like a web, held together by the compelling and persuasive Christian vision of reality. They are snapshots, part of a greater panorama.

That's why we can't see the doctrine of the atonement in isolation. It is connected with so many other leading themes of the Christian faith, such as the nature of God, the identity of Jesus of Nazareth, and the Christian understanding of human nature. The 'big picture' of faith is all about who we really are, what is really wrong with us and the world, what God proposes to do about this, and what we must do in response. The doctrine of the atonement is one piece in that jigsaw, joined up to other pieces. It's pointless to ask which comes first. They all come together and belong together, as the grand vision of the Christian faith.

So let's sketch the ideas that we will explore in this chapter. We can think of the doctrine of the atonement as a node on the spider's web of faith, a point at which multiple strands of theological silk converge and connect with each other. That's what gives a web its strength and allows it to hold together. One of these strands is the loving purpose of the God who created the world. Another is the realization that human nature is wounded, damaged and broken. It needs to be fixed, healed and repaired. But we can't do this ourselves. It lies beyond us. We need a saviour, someone who is the solution to our problem, not part of it. A third strand is the doctrine of the Incarnation, which affirms both that God is with us and that a redeemer has entered the world. The person who went to the cross and died there was no ordinary human being. His death thus had a deeper, extraordinary meaning.

But enough by way of introduction. Let's begin to explore the theme of atonement in a little more detail.[1]

Theories of the atonement

When I was about eight, my form teacher at school asked everyone in our class to write a short essay on the greatest human invention. Most of my friends chose entirely sensible things, like antibiotics and electricity. For some reason I can't quite remember, I suggested that one of the best things ever invented was the deodorant. Perhaps a little unwisely, I then went on to suggest that my form teacher had yet to make use of this wonderful invention. That was how I came to discover the meaning of the word 'detention'.

As I've got older, I've come to appreciate the wonder of many other things. I now think one of the greatest human inventions is the rewind button. When I watch movies like *Mission Impossible* or *The Matrix*, I often find I have to rewind. Why? Because I've lost the plot, or failed to appreciate the significance of an event that took place earlier on in the film. Being able to zoom back allows me to try to make more sense of what is happening. The only problem is that it now takes me twice as long as anyone else to watch a movie!

There's a serious point here. It is very easy for us to overlook points of importance, or to fail to grasp the deeper significance of something that truly matters. We see something, but don't realize its significance. Or we read something, and think we've understood it, only to discover later that we missed what was really important. That's why we need to read the Gospel story of Jesus of Nazareth again and again. We miss lots of things the first time round!

In this chapter, we are focusing on the meaning of the crucifixion and resurrection of Jesus. We're going to try and tease out the significance and relevance of the cross of Christ. Let me suggest a few ground rules to guide us as we think about this.

First, we must never think that the significance of Jesus is related only to the mechanics of securing salvation, though that's certainly the impression some theologians give when they talk about 'theories of the atonement'. Securing salvation is part of the Christian picture. But it's only part of it.

For a start, we have to take into account that much Christian devotion is focused on the person of Jesus. Bernard of Clairvaux's great twelfth-century hymn captures this well:

> Jesus, the very thought of Thee
> With sweetness fills the breast;
> But sweeter far Thy face to see,
> And in Thy presence rest.

Theories, which are really ways of seeing things, as C. S. Lewis points out, are useful in that they help to highlight things and bring them into sharper focus. But a theory can never be a substitute for the thing itself. Theories try to describe reality – but they are not themselves that reality.

There is a middle way between musing on abstract theories about Jesus and focusing on personal devotion to him. It is easy to dismiss the former as a form of dogmatism and the latter as a form of pietism. Yet when properly grasped, each can enrich the other. Doctrine can deepen our appreciation of Jesus of Nazareth, and hence increase our devotion to him. Reflection on the person of Jesus – as we see, for example, in his encounters with people in the Gospels – can prevent us from falling into some abstract way of thinking about Jesus. Jesus must be an object of our adoration, not merely a theological puzzle we try to understand.

And second, we must never treat the death of Jesus on the cross in isolation from his life and resurrection. It is no accident that most Christian churches recognize three days of particular significance in the year: Christmas (when we celebrate Christ's birth, and think about the doctrine of the Incarnation); Good Friday (when we recall Christ's death on the cross, and think about the doctrine of the atonement); and Easter Day (when we think about Christ's resurrection and the doctrine of Christian hope). Each of these is part of the opulent Gospel witness to the meaning of Jesus, and all can enrich our understanding and strengthen our devotion.

The theme of incarnation thus underpins our thinking about the meaning of the cross. If Jesus were an ordinary human being, we could interpret the cross in a number of ways – such as a tragic miscarriage of justice, or an ideal of self-giving love. But if Jesus of Nazareth is God incarnate, then the cross calls out to be understood as representing a crossing of the ways of God and the ways of human beings. It is a place with both vertical and horizontal axes, where the story of God and the story of humanity intersect.

The unusual word 'atonement' has already come up several times in our discussion, but I haven't yet explained what it means. The English word can be traced back to the sixteenth century when William Tyndale used it in his ground-breaking English translation of the New Testament (1526). Tyndale found himself encountering some difficulty in conveying the concept of 'reconciliation' to his readers (in that this now-familiar English word 'reconciliation' had yet to be invented). The idea, however, was clearly present in the New Testament. So how could it be expressed in English? How could anyone talk about 'reconciliation' when English words like 'reconciliation' or 'reconcile' had not yet been coined?

Tyndale solved the problem by minting the word 'atonement' to express the state of 'at-one-ment' – that is, reconciliation – between God and humanity as a result of the death of Jesus of Nazareth. Tyndale's translation was so influential that this hitherto unfamiliar word gained growing acceptance, and was used in perhaps the most celebrated English Bible of all time – the King James Bible of 1611: 'We also joy in God through our Lord Jesus Christ, by whom we have now received the atonement' (Romans 5.11). This suggested that the benefits won by Christ through his cross and resurrection could be summarized in the phrase 'the atonement'. And so the term passed into wider use. 'Atonement' has come to mean something like 'the benefits that Jesus won by his life, death and resurrection'.

In what follows, we shall try to make sense of the death of Jesus of Nazareth on the cross by following the trails left by the earliest Christians in the New Testament, as they tried to find words and images capable of expressing the new world of life and thought opened up by his resurrection. We'll begin with one of the most dramatic themes of the New Testament – the victory of Jesus of Nazareth over sin and death.

Victory over sin and death

'Thanks be to God, who gives us the victory through our Lord Jesus Christ' (1 Corinthians 15.57). The early Church exulted in the triumph of Christ at Calvary over sin, death and Satan. The powerful imagery of the triumphant Christ rising from the dead and being installed as 'ruler of all' (Greek: *pantokrator*) seized the imagination of the Christian east. The cross was seen as the site of a famous battle, comparable to the great Homeric epics, in which the forces of good and evil fought and the good emerged victorious.

There was rather more interest in proclaiming Jesus's victory over the enemies of humanity than in speculating precisely how it came about. Early Christian liturgies were saturated with the thought of the cosmic victory achieved by Jesus on the cross. His resurrection and triumphant opening of the gates of heaven to believers were proclaimed and celebrated, rather than made the focus of theological debate.

There is ample historical evidence that the first Christians lived out their hope in the face of persecution and opposition. Christianity was an illegal religion until the conversion of the Roman emperor Constantine in the year 313. Christians were regularly martyred for their faith. Roman commentators often noted how Christians met their deaths with remarkable bravery and courage, and wondered why. The answer is clear:

because of the death and resurrection of Jesus of Nazareth, death had become a gateway to the New Jerusalem. It was no longer to be feared.

Some Christian thinkers visualized the triumph of Jesus over death and sin through the cross and resurrection as a victory parade comparable to those of ancient Rome. In its classical form, a general's soldiers, often leading the chain-bound leaders of the cities or countries they had defeated, went ahead of the victorious military leader through the streets of Rome, preparing the way for his triumphant arrival at the temple of Jupiter on the Capitoline Hill.

It was a small step for Christian writers to encourage believers to think of the risen Jesus exultantly processing through the world, leading his conquered enemies – such as sin and death – behind him. Such powerful symbolism was firmly grounded in the New Testament, which spoke of the risen Jesus as making captivity a captive (Ephesians 4.8).

This theme can be seen in the art of this early period and, more easily, in hymns such as the great Easter anthem 'The royal banners forward go', written by Venantius Honorius Clementianus Fortunatus (*c.* 530–*c.* 610):

> The royal banners forward go,
> The cross shines forth in mystic glow;
> Where he in flesh, our flesh Who made,
> Our sentence bore, our ransom paid.

A further development of the theme of 'Christ the victor' depicts Christ as extending the triumph of the cross and resurrection to the realm of the dead. The medieval idea of 'the harrowing of hell' holds that, after dying upon the cross, Christ descended to hell, and broke down its gates in order that the souls imprisoned there might go free. The idea rests (rather tenuously, it has to be said) upon a biblical text (1 Peter 3.18–22) which refers to Christ making 'a proclamation to the spirits in prison'. The dramatic power of this scene was such that, despite its slightly questionable theological foundation, it was picked up and incorporated into countless popular accounts of the significance of Easter. The hymn 'Ye choirs of New Jerusalem', written by Fulbert of Chartres (*c.* 970–1028), expresses this idea in two of its verses: Christ, as the 'lion of Judah' (Revelation 5.5), has by his death and resurrection defeated Satan, the serpent (Genesis 3.15):

> For Judah's Lion bursts his chains,
> Crushing the serpent's head;
> And cries aloud through death's domains
> To wake the imprisoned dead.
>
> Devouring depths of hell their prey
> At his command restore;
> His ransomed hosts pursue their way
> Where Jesus goes before.

C. S. Lewis wove this thread of theological reflection into *The Lion, the Witch and the Wardrobe*. Remember, the book tells the story of Narnia, a land which is discovered accidentally by four children rummaging around in an old wardrobe. They soon encounter the White Witch, who keeps the land of Narnia covered in a perpetual wintry snow. We discover that she rules Narnia not as a matter of right, but by stealth and deception. The true ruler of the land is absent; in his absence, the witch has subjected it to oppression, imprisoning many of Narnia's inhabitants as stone statues in her castle.

As the narrative moves on, we discover that the rightful ruler of the land is the great and noble lion Aslan. As Aslan advances into Narnia to reclaim his kingdom, winter gives way to spring, and the snow begins to melt. The witch realizes that her power is beginning to fade, and puts Aslan to death on a stone table. Lewis's description of the resurrection of Aslan is one of his more tender passages, evoking both the deep sense of sorrow evident in the New Testament accounts of the burial of Christ, and joyful recognition of the reality of his resurrection. Yet Aslan defeats death, and ends its baleful rule. Lewis then describes how Aslan – 'the lion of Judah, who has burst his chains' – breaks into the witch's castle, breathes upon the statues and restores them to life, before leading this liberated army through the shattered gates of the once great fortress to freedom.

We might ask quite a reasonable question here. If the death and resurrection of Jesus are a victory over sin and death, why do they remain part of our lives? What kind of victory can we possibly be we talking about?

I remember changing flights at Changi airport in Singapore on my way from London to Australia in the early 1990s, and getting into a conversation with an elderly fellow passenger. This old man told me that the Changi area of Singapore had been the site of a Japanese prisoner-of-war camp during the Second World War. He himself had been a prisoner there and, as a result, always felt distressed when passing through the airport. It brought back many traumatic memories.

The man described the bleakness of camp life, and the virtual absence of hope. Then he told me how one of the prisoners, who owned an illegal short-wave radio, had heard a news broadcast in the middle of 1945: it stated that the Japanese war effort had collapsed as a result of some new kind of bomb being used by the Allies. The news travelled through the camp like wildfire. Although the prisoners were still captive, they knew that the enemy had been beaten and it was only a matter of time before they were released. I was told they began to laugh and cry as if they were already free, though that freedom was still a matter of hope and promise rather than an actual reality.

I hope you find this illustration helpful in thinking about the meaning of the cross and resurrection. Sin and death remain realities in our world. But their power has been broken. We live and struggle on in hope. We know what the final outcome of the battle will be, even though it still rages around us.

Entering God's presence: the cross as sacrifice

The New Testament speaks of the death of Jesus of Nazareth on the cross as a sacrifice. What does this mean? To the modern age, the notion of sacrifice seems strange and distant. A chess player might speak of sacrificing a pawn in order to gain a tactical advantage over his opponent. A busy manager might decide to sacrifice her lunch break in order to finish a project on time. In each case, the term 'sacrifice' really means giving something up. Yet it is clear that the Old Testament uses the word in a very different sense.

We must remember that the first Christians were deeply immersed in the language, ideas and practices of Judaism. Jesus of Nazareth was the fulfilment of the hopes and aspirations of Israel. It made perfect sense to think of Jesus' death as a sacrifice, along the lines of the sacrifices offered in the Temple at Jerusalem. Yet this was not about a repetition, or even an extension, of Israel's religious system. It was about bringing it to fulfilment – with such effectiveness that it was no longer required.

An example of the use of sacrificial ideas and images to make sense of the identity of Jesus of Nazareth is found in John the Baptist's declaration that Jesus is 'the Lamb of God who takes away the sin of the world' (John 1.29). This image calls to mind the great Passover celebrations of Israel, when a lamb would be slain as a reminder of God's faithfulness in delivering his people from captivity in Egypt (Exodus 12). Speaking of Jesus in this way suggests that the people of God are in captivity to sin, and need a new act of redemption and deliverance to set them free from its bonds.

The image of Jesus as the 'the Lamb of God, who takes away the sin of the world' also taps into the prophecy of Isaiah, who spoke of a coming suffering servant who would be slain like a lamb, for his people (Isaiah 53). This suffering servant of God would be 'wounded for our transgressions, crushed for our iniquities' (Isaiah 53.5). This prophecy of Christ compares him to 'a lamb that is led to the slaughter' (Isaiah 53.7), on whom the guilt and sin of the world is laid. (There may also be an affinity with the scapegoat (Leviticus 16.21–22), which was sent into the wilderness bearing the sin of God's people.)

We see here a theme about the human predicament that plays an important role in Christian thinking about the meaning of the cross: exclusion from the presence of God. There is a fundamental breach in the relationship between God and humanity on account of sin. We need to be purified and sanctified before we can hope to see and approach God. Access to God depended on the purity of the individual. Guilt and sin had to be purged before it was possible to enter into the presence of God.

Two Old Testament passages echo this theme with particular force. The first is the Genesis account of the Fall, which ends with the expulsion of Adam and Eve from Eden (Genesis 3.24). There would be no going back to the garden. Intimacy with God was a thing of the past. Yet writers such as Augustine of Hippo argue that we retain a distant memory of Eden, and a hope that we might one day return – both to paradise, and to fellowship with God.[2]

The second passage is the account of the 'Day of Atonement' (Leviticus 16), which depicts Israel's high priest making an annual sacrifice on behalf of the nation. This solemn ritual reminded Israel that God alone could cleanse her from her sin. We should not be surprised that the New Testament framed its understanding of the significance of Christ's death using language and imagery borrowed from the solemnities of Israel's worship – the 'holy of holies', the Temple, its altar and sacrifices, and the ritual washing away of sin through blood sacrifice.

Access to God was understood to require a state of purity. However, we need to make a distinction between 'being impure or unclean' and 'being sinful'. Burying the dead was seen within Jewish culture as a necessary and charitable action. Yet anyone burying a dead person would have to touch the corpse, which would make him unclean (but not sinful). If someone who had buried a corpse wanted to enter the sacred space of the Temple afterwards, he would first need to undergo a purification ritual. In the same way, 'being pure' is not the same as 'being without sin', even though the ideas are similar. The New Testament holds that the life, death and resurrection of Jesus of Nazareth breaks down both barriers to entering the presence of God, by abolishing the need for ritual cleanliness on the one hand, and by purging the guilt of sin on the other.

What we find in the New Testament is not really an extended and detailed theory of Jesus's death as a sacrifice. Rather, we see the language and imagery of sacrifice used to affirm that Jesus actually achieved what sacrifices were meant to. Guilt and impurity were removed. The most extended discussion of the theme is found in the letter to the Hebrews, which develops the illuminating and important idea that Jesus is both a perfect high priest and a perfect sacrificial victim, so that his sacrifice is 'once for all' – that is, something that never needs to be repeated. In other words, Jesus has made the cultic system of Israel redundant by achieving for Christians what it promised, but did not deliver.

There is therefore no longer any need for priests, sacrifices or temples in the Christian vision of life. Jesus has accomplished something so significant and important that it obviates the need for the Old Testament religious cult, even if its language and images remain helpful in understanding his triumph. Christians thus use imagery from Israel's past to make sense of the Christian present.

This caused few problems in New Testament times, when many were familiar with sacrifice, both as an idea and a practice, in the religious traditions of Rome, Athens and Israel. Yet as the Christian Church became increasingly distant from the ideas and practices of Judaism, the idea of sacrifice needed explanation, as its imagery became less and less familiar. Many Christians today find older ways of speaking about the sacrificial death of Christ puzzling, if not alienating. For example, consider this section of a nineteenth-century hymn, based on Revelation 7.14.

> Are you washed in the blood,
> In the soul-cleansing blood of the Lamb?
> Are your garments spotless? Are they white as snow?
> Are you washed in the blood of the Lamb?

Many now find this imagery incomprehensible, even repulsive. Perhaps for this reason, recent Christian writings have focused on communicating the significance of the cross as a sacrifice, rather than emphasizing its bloody imagery.

> After agreeing to baptize him along with the sinners, John the Baptist looked at Jesus and pointed him out as the 'Lamb of God, who takes away the sin of the world'. By doing so, he reveals that Jesus is at the same time the suffering Servant who silently allows himself to be led to the slaughter and who bears the sin of the multitudes, and also the Paschal Lamb, the symbol of Israel's redemption at the first Passover. Christ's whole life expresses his mission: 'to serve, and to give his life as a ransom for many.'[3]

Let's move on and look at another aspect of the death of Jesus on the cross – the idea that his death is a 'ransom'. What does this mean?

Ransom

Unfortunately, the concept of 'ransom' is as familiar to us today as it was in the ancient world. People continue to be kidnapped and held to ransom, with money demanded to secure their freedom. The more important the prisoner, the greater the ransom likely to be required. In the end, the amount paid to secure a loved one's freedom may reflect how much that person is valued and esteemed. (Of course, some people are strongly opposed to giving in to kidnappers' demands, whatever the consequences of this might be.)

In the Old Testament, when the people of Jerusalem are exiled in Babylon, God speaks of ransoming them from their captivity by handing over some of the ancient world's greatest nations in exchange. 'For I am the LORD your God, the Holy One of Israel, your Saviour. I give Egypt as your ransom, Ethiopia and Seba in exchange for you' (Isaiah 43.3).

It is not surprising that the New Testament should use this image as a natural and powerful way of expressing the significance of Jesus' death on the cross. It is a 'ransom for all' (1 Timothy 2.6). Most significantly, the Gospels indicate that this specific word is used by Jesus himself to refer to the meaning of his own forthcoming death: 'For the Son of Man came not to be served but to serve, and to give his life a ransom for many' (Mark 10.45).

The concept of ransom appeals to our imaginations because it is accessible and doesn't need explanation. But we will still benefit from considering it from various angles.

To start with, let's reflect on the context that the image of ransom presupposes. Someone has been captured. He is being held against his will. He is trapped, and cannot break free. His freedom depends utterly on the willingness of someone else to meet the demands of his kidnappers.

This frames the Christian understanding of salvation. We are trapped in a web of sin. We've fallen into a pit, and can't get out. We are ensnared. Many scholars see this theme as lying at the heart of Paul's analysis of his predicament:

> I do not understand my own actions. For I do not do what I want, but I do the very thing I hate . . . But in fact it is no longer I that do it, but sin that dwells within me . . . For I do not do the good I want, but the evil I do not want is what I do. Now if I do what I do not want, it is no longer I that do it, but sin that dwells within me . . . Wretched man that I am! Who will rescue me from this body of death? Thanks be to God through Jesus Christ our Lord! (Romans 7.15–25)

Second, a ransom is a price paid to secure liberation. This might take the form of money, possessions or territories. But in every case, the point is that freedom does not come easily. We have neither the power nor the resources to liberate ourselves. Someone else has to set us free as an expression of their love and commitment to us. We are to think of Jesus as someone precious and valuable, handed over so that we might be released.

This is a prominent theme in Paul's letter to the Christian church at Corinth. Christians, he declared, 'were bought with a price' (1 Corinthians 6.20; 7.23). The same idea lies behind the image of 'redemption', used frequently by Paul as a way of illuminating what Jesus achieved on the cross (Romans 3.24; 8.23). To redeem someone is to buy that person back from bondage, whether this servitude was imposed or chosen. The ancient world had a thriving slave trade, and some people were forced to sell themselves into servitude as a way of paying off debts. To redeem a slave was to bring about a radical change in the slave's status: that individual was no longer someone's possession, but a free person. We have been ransomed 'with the precious blood of Christ, like that of a lamb without defect or blemish' (1 Peter 1.18–19). In other words, there has been a radical transformation in our status and way of life as a result of Jesus's death on the cross.

And finally, the image of ransom speaks of liberation. When the ransom is paid, the prisoners regain their liberty. They are set free from bondage. The prison doors are thrown open. Once more, this chimes in with one of the great themes of the New Testament. Jesus brings freedom – freedom from bondage to the law, bondage to sin, and bondage to the fear of death. Through his sacrifice, Jesus is able to 'free those who all their lives were held in slavery by the fear of death'

(Hebrews 2.15). 'The creation itself will be set free from its bondage to decay and will obtain the freedom of the glory of the children of God' (Romans 8.21).

The demonstration of divine love

Everyone loves a page-turner. I think I was about ten years old when I read Sir Arthur Conan Doyle's *The Lost World*. This novel, published in 1912, was a precursor to *Jurassic Park* and other adventure stories dealing with lost (or recreated) worlds inhabited by dinosaurs. A London journalist, Edward Malone, sets off with an eccentric professor to explore a mysterious raised plateau in South America, and has lots of adventures with dinosaurs.

But why did he do this? Because the woman he loved thought he was far too boring. If he really loved her, she declared, he would have to do something bold, dangerous and *interesting* to prove it. Actions speak louder than words. She wanted to marry a hero! So after fending off countless dinosaurs and hostile tribes in South America, Malone returned to London, only to find that the woman he had loved had got bored in his absence, and had married a rather dull bank clerk instead.

What we do shows what we are like. The Christian gospel speaks of a God who loves us, and who shows this love by acting. Earlier, we noted C. S. Lewis's image of God as a diver, who plunges into the depths of cold, murky, muddy water to retrieve a precious object – namely, humanity. It's a memorable image of someone doing something dangerous because they want to save something that's important to them. It's a theme that we find in the New Testament. God is love – and God shows that love by sending Jesus of Nazareth into the world as an atoning sacrifice for sin (1 John 4.9–10).

In his poem 'The Dear Bargain', Richard Crashaw (1612–49) reflects on the astonishingly high value placed on people by Jesus. Like Paul, Crashaw found it difficult to grasp why Jesus died for sinners. You could understand a person laying down his or her life for someone really important (Romans 5.7). But for those as ordinary as us?

> Lord, what is man? Why should he cost Thee
>   So dear? What hath his ruin lost Thee?
> Lord, what is man, that Thou hast over-bought
>   So much a thing of nought?

Crashaw here picks up a leading theme of the New Testament: 'God proves his love for us in that while we still were sinners Christ died for us' (Romans 5.8). A loving God acts in love to make salvation possible in and through Jesus of Nazareth and invites us to return this love in response. 'For God so loved the world that he gave his only Son, so that everyone who believes in him may not perish but may have eternal life' (John 3.16).

Some preachers occasionally suggest that Jesus's death on the cross changes God's character; that the angry and unforgiving God of the Old Testament is displaced by the compassionate God of the New. But this is not so. The cross expresses the way God is, and always has been – loving, gracious and righteous. God's chosen way of saving humanity weaves together divine justice, love, mercy and compassion in ways we can never fully understand.

Forgiveness of sin

Finally, we turn to the great theme of forgiveness. The death of Jesus of Nazareth makes forgiveness possible. This theological insight is deeply embedded in popular Christian piety, such as the well-known Good Friday hymn 'There is a green hill':

> He died that we might be forgiven,
> He died to make us good,
> that we might go at last to heaven,
> saved by his precious blood.
>
> There was no other good enough
> to pay the price of sin;
> He only could unlock the gate
> of heaven, and let us in.

The death of Christ is the basis of our forgiveness – a powerful reminder of its costliness and reality.

The great theme of a loving God who forgives people is movingly portrayed in the parable of the prodigal son (Luke 15.11–32), with its vivid depiction of the waiting father who rushes out to greet his wayward boy. But the story also raises an awkward question for many people. How can the father just forgive his son like that? It seems to suggest that the past can be forgotten as if it never happened or didn't really matter. We often find that our sympathies lie with the older brother, who is both hurt and outraged by his father's behaviour.

And we are surely right to be worried here. It's easy to cheapen forgiveness. I could say 'I forgive you' to someone who has deeply hurt me, and not really mean it. My resentment against that person would remain, and I would have 'forgiven' him or her in word only, not in reality. But let's remember that this parable only illuminates some of the aspects of God's forgiveness of our sins. There is more that needs to be said.

In terms of our relationship with God, the cross brings home to us the deep hurt, offence and pain we have caused.

God is angered by our sin, and in Christ, makes clear how painful and costly true forgiveness really is by demonstrating how serious sin is in the first place. The offer of forgiveness of our sins is both deeply humiliating and deeply satisfying. It is humiliating, because it forces us to recognize and acknowledge how far short we fall; it is satisfying, because the very offer of forgiveness implies that we matter to God. To put it very simply: God wants to be friends with us again. And for that reason, Jesus 'suffered for sins once for all, the righteous for the unrighteous, in order to bring you to God' (1 Peter 3.18).

Real forgiveness is not an easy thing to encounter, because to accept an offer of forgiveness is to admit to ourselves and the other party involved that we have done something for which we need to be forgiven. Of course, it may even be that we are unaware of the hurt and pain we've caused by our actions to those who we love.

God's forgiveness is both about liberation from the power of sin and about living the kind of life that God wants. We'll look at this in more detail in the next chapter. The point is that Jesus models the redeemed life. Not only does he make this new life possible; he also shows us what we are meant to be like, rather than merely telling us what we ought to be like. Just as Jesus forgave those who crucified him, so we ought to forgive those who offend or oppress us. God's forgiveness of our sins can release in us the generosity of spirit we need to forgive the sins of others. As C. S. Lewis put it, 'To be a Christian means to forgive the inexcusable because God has forgiven the inexcusable in you.'[4]

Now there's more that needs to be said about how forgiveness is established and mediated through the death of Jesus on the cross. We need to ask: what is meant or implied by the declaration, which we noted earlier, that Jesus 'himself bore our sins in his body on the cross, so that, free from sins, we might live for righteousness; by his wounds you have been healed' (1 Peter 2.24)?

The New Testament writers saw a clear parallel between the suffering and death of Jesus and the figure in the Old Testament often referred to by scholars as the 'suffering servant'. This mysterious figure is presented as a sin-bearer – someone who takes on our burdens of guilt, impurity, punishment and illness – though no explanation is provided of how this process takes place. Let us remind ourselves of one of the most evocative descriptions of this figure.

> Surely he has borne our infirmities and carried our diseases; yet we accounted him stricken, struck down by God, and afflicted. But he was wounded for our transgressions, crushed for our iniquities; upon him was the punishment that made us whole, and by his bruises we are healed. All we like sheep have gone astray; we have all turned to our own way, and the LORD has laid on him the iniquity of us all.
>
> (Isaiah 53.4–6)

The New Testament doesn't offer a detailed theoretical explanation of how Jesus bore our sins: that's something that later theologians tried to develop, though in doing so they were going beyond the cautious statements of the New Testament itself. What the New Testament does say is something along these lines: 'We don't quite understand how this happened. But it did. And it fits into a pattern of God's dealings with Israel.' What Jesus achieved on the cross thus brings to fulfilment some of the great themes and aspirations of the Old Testament. Looking back now, we can appreciate that God has acted just as we would expect, in faithful accordance with his promises, showing both mercy and righteousness.

But the really important thing is this: real sin has been really forgiven. We may struggle to grasp how this has happened, or could happen. But salvation does not depend on our understanding of the process by which it is possible. An illustration might help here.

When I was young, I developed a bad infection which had to be treated with antibiotics. I took penicillin as directed by my doctor, and the infection quickly cleared up. I hadn't the slightest idea what penicillin was, or how it worked. I just trusted the doctor's diagnosis and the cure he prescribed.

Many years later, as an Oxford undergraduate studying chemistry, I attended a course of lectures on the effects of drugs on living organisms. I discovered that penicillin destroys bacteria. But the drug had worked perfectly well for me a decade or more earlier, though I hadn't understood exactly what was happening at the time.

The cross is a 'mystery', in the proper sense of that word – it is something we can never fully grasp. But though we don't entirely understand how it works, we trust that it does. One of the favourite hymns of the nineteenth century was penned by Joseph Hart (1712–68). Though rarely sung now, it was widely appreciated for its strong statement of trust in the saving power of the cross:

> The moment a sinner believes,
> And trusts in his crucified Lord,
> His pardon at once he receives,
> Redemption in full through his blood.

How does this happen? What is the inner logic of this process of transformation? Hart didn't really care. The all-important point was that Christ's death on the cross, embraced through faith, was able to bring about the transformation of our situation. Like penicillin, it worked. Others could worry about the theory. For Hart, all that mattered was trusting that Jesus had done whatever needed to be done – and done it well. Some will sympathize with him at this point! But part of our 'discipleship of the mind' is to try and go beneath the surface of our faith, and explore and appreciate its deeper structure and logic.

In this chapter, we have looked at a number of New Testament snapshots which capture aspects of the significance of the cross and help us put together a more panoramic vision. But there are still many questions. For a start, how do we connect up with Jesus of Nazareth? How can we benefit from something that happened far, far away, and long, long ago? And what difference do the life, death and resurrection of Jesus make to us? In the final chapter, we will explore these themes.

5

Jesus of Nazareth and the life of faith

————————•◦•————————

I suppose it was inevitable that I would become a stamp collector when I was young. My father had begun collecting stamps in the 1930s (I still have his first stamp album). So I began to collect them as well. By the age of 13, I was well on the way to becoming an expert on the watermarks of British postage stamps issued during the reign of Edward VII. Curiously, nobody else I met at school seemed in the slightest bit interested in this topic. In fact, they all thought it was unspeakably dull and irrelevant. My best friend at school at the time used to shake his head in despair. 'Why can't you get interested in something worthwhile – like football?'

For many people, theology is like stamp collecting – interesting to some, but without any real relevance to the business of everyday human life. You stick theological theories into your stamp album, close the covers, and forget about them until the next time you open it. They make no difference to real life. They're just things you collect, and look at occasionally.

Yet the New Testament doesn't allow us to think in this way. The life, death and resurrection of Jesus of Nazareth are presented as transformative, changing the way we live. Our personal and social worlds are changed, and are meant to be changed, by Jesus.

Let's give an example. One of our theological postage stamps might be the belief that Jesus is Lord. Jesus of Nazareth is the one who we trust, follow and obey. When the German churches refused to conform to Nazism in the 1930s, they took their stand on the lordship of Christ: 'Jesus Christ, as he is attested for us in Holy Scripture, is the one Word of God which we have to hear and which we have to trust and obey in life and in death.' Some object to any idea of lordship, seeing this as contrary to individual freedom. It's not. It's about choosing who we believe we can trust. It's about choosing to commit ourselves to the care of the 'Good Shepherd', who journeys with us as we travel through life, supporting and sustaining us.

Let's look at another key element in any understanding of Jesus of Nazareth – that he is our Saviour. We've already looked at how we can make sense of this theme, and how it fits into a 'big picture' of the identity and significance of Jesus. But what difference does it make? A lot. A favourite sermon illustration for salvation used in the Middle Ages drew its inspiration from passages such as Psalm 40.2: '[the Lord] drew me up from the desolate pit, out of the miry bog, and set my feet upon a rock.'

The human predicament is likened to being trapped in a deep pit. We have fallen in, broken a leg, and are now unable to climb out. We are stuck in deep mud, and every time we try to get out, we sink deeper into the slime. Our hopes rest on someone climbing down into the pit and carrying us out. Or someone taking hold of our hand and pulling us out of the treacherous mud. Without a saviour, we are in a hopeless situation. But the coming of a saviour is about the hope of rescue. The New Testament declares first that there *is* a saviour, and second, that this long-awaited saviour is Jesus of Nazareth.

Why is Jesus of Nazareth central to the Christian faith?

One of the questions that perplexed me as I hovered around the borderlands of faith in the early 1970s was this. How could someone who lived two thousand years ago be of any relevance today? I was a scientist, and my reasoning went along these lines: if the answer's right, (a) you don't need to rely on the person who found it and (b) it doesn't depend on the person who found it. The answer and the person who discovered it can be separated from each other.

After all, if Isaac Newton hadn't discovered gravity back in the seventeenth century, someone else would have done so instead. If Copernicus hadn't figured out that the earth went around the sun, another bright spark would have come to this conclusion sooner or later. Sure, Newton and Copernicus got there first. But if an idea is right, it has a life of its own.

Jesus of Nazareth had some good ideas. But were they dependent on him? The Christian emphasis on the centrality of Jesus didn't make sense to me all those years ago. If Jesus was like Newton or Copernicus, he would simply have been the channel for ideas that could survive perfectly well without him. He was the medium for a message that was essentially independent of him.

Now as I later discovered, I was completely wrong about this. But I was wrong in an interesting way which helps cast light on the unique role that Jesus of Nazareth plays within the Christian faith. Given who Jesus is, his coming itself is immensely significant. It is not simply that he tells us something useful. The very act of coming to be with us is part of the message. 'The Word became flesh and lived among us' (John 1.14).

Imagine an ancient realm, ruled by a royal family that has little interest in its subjects other than as a useful source of income. Then a new king comes to power. He is different. He cares about his people and wants the best for them. He issues a royal proclamation of his compassion for his subjects, then leaves his palace and goes to live alongside them, sharing their joys, pain and sorrow. Do you see the point? What the king does is part of his message. He enters their situation as an expression of his commitment to his people; he dwells where they dwell.

It's not a great analogy, but it helped me grasp the inter-connectedness of the message and messenger in Jesus of Nazareth. This idea is found throughout the letters of the New Testament but perhaps most clearly in the first letter of John, which sets two statements beside each other as if they were two sides of the same coin: 'God is love' (1 John 4.8) and 'God's love was revealed among us in this way: God sent his only Son into the world so that we might live through him' (1 John 4.9). The point being made is that God's identity is expressed in God's actions. What God does, mirrors and expresses who God is. 'The Word became flesh' is thus an intrinsic part of the good news of the gospel. Message and messenger are inseparable.

But there is more to it than this. As we saw in a previous chapter, Jesus of Nazareth is our Saviour – the one who makes possible the transformation of the human situation.

But how does this transformation come about? Quite simply, it happens as our relationship with Christ deepens. The New Testament uses a range of images to help us make sense of this – such as Jesus inhabiting us, or the Spirit remoulding us after the likeness of Jesus. As we accept Jesus of Nazareth as our Lord, abide in him and suffer with him, so we begin on the journey to being glorified with him. For Jesus is not simply the foundation of our salvation; he is also its goal. The Christian hope of heaven is about being in the presence of the risen Christ.

In his sermon 'The Weight of Glory', preached at Oxford in June 1941, C. S. Lewis pointed out that there are different kinds of reward. One kind of reward 'has no natural connection with the things you do to earn it, and is quite foreign to the desires that ought to accompany those things'. Yet Lewis argues that 'proper rewards are not simply tacked on to the activity for which they are given, but are the activity itself in consummation.' It is a powerful and illuminating conclusion, which Lewis illustrates with characteristic clarity. Imagine a young boy learning ancient Greek. His goal? To be able to read the works of the great classical writer Sophocles. (That young boy, by the way, was Lewis himself.) We could easily extend this: someone might long to play the piano really well so she could perform Beethoven's Moonlight Sonata; a young tennis player might be inspired to train day and night so that he could win Wimbledon.

In these examples, the point is simple: what is there to be gained is the natural outcome of what is being done. The prize is the consummation of the process, not something arbitrarily tacked on. The goal consummates the journey that led to it in the first place.

And that's what we need to grasp about the Christian vision of salvation. Christ makes it possible for us to know him, to pray to him, to draw close to him in times of need and despair, and he will finally raise us up to where he now is. Redemption is a deepened and transfigured enriching of our present relationship with Jesus of Nazareth, by which what has been begun in this life is fulfilled and extended. As Lewis put it, Christians know that heaven is the 'consummation of their earthly discipleship'.

In the light of this discussion, it's easy to see why Jesus of Nazareth is not analogous to Isaac Newton or anyone else. Jesus of Nazareth is the source of our true knowledge, the foundation of our salvation, and the goal of our lives. There are three points that we should make here.

First, Jesus of Nazareth is the ground of our redemption, in that his death and resurrection throw open the door that leads to eternal life and salvation. These benefits can be obtained in no other way and through no other person. Meditating on the cross, as we have seen, is one of the ways of appreciating the costliness of the privileges we have been granted through Christ.

Second, Jesus is the guarantor of our redemption, in that his death and resurrection demonstrate the total reliability of the God who promises to see us through from death to eternal life. In Jesus, 'every one of God's promises is a "Yes"' (2 Corinthians 1.20).

And third, Jesus of Nazareth is the final goal of our journey of faith. Where Christ has gone, we shall follow. He has been glorified, and we gladly and patiently await the promise of being clothed in his glory. This is why so many passages in the New Testament urge their readers to raise their eyes heavenward (Philippians 3.13–14; Hebrews 12.2), in order that we may regain a sense of wonder and anticipation of finally arriving at journey's end, where Jesus awaits us with open arms.

This emphasis on the importance of Jesus naturally raises another question, to which we now turn. How do we connect up with him?

Connecting up: more reflections on the nature of faith

I've always been struck by a phrase I came across years ago in the writings of Richard Hooker (1554–1600), one of the great English theologians of the Elizabethan age: 'Faith is the only hand which putteth on Christ.'[1] Hooker is here concerned more with what faith does, than with what it is. What is the function of faith? What is its effect? His answer is simple: to 'put on Christ'. Hooker speaks of Jesus of Nazareth being like a splendid garment, which amply clothes us – both protecting us from the cold and hiding our shame. And what God provides, we are invited to receive and use.

Another favourite image from the Middle Ages was to think of believers – whether male or female – as being married to Jesus.[2] This solemn, committed relationship highlighted the importance of mutual love and a covenanted bond between the believer and Christ. In any marriage, the bride and groom share everything that they possess. In the spiritual marriage between Jesus and the believer, the believer shares in the 'benefits of Christ' – namely, salvation, forgiveness and eternal life, the trophies won by Jesus through his obedience on the cross. Jesus receives our sin and shame – and takes them away from us. A living and loving relationship with Jesus is thus the framework which makes sense of the removal of our guilt, and our receiving of his righteousness.

In more contemporary terms, we can think of connecting up with Jesus of Nazareth as being like accepting an offer of forgiveness or friendship; receiving a gift; taking medicine; or becoming part of a bigger story. Let's begin by thinking about forgiveness and friendship.

Imagine you have had a major falling out with a close friend. Harsh words have been said. The relationship is damaged. What's to be done? You may offer your apologies though that doesn't mean they will be accepted. But in reaching out, you are taking the initiative in trying to restore the relationship. Similarly God, from whom we have been estranged and alienated (Colossians 1.21–22), comes in search of us, offering to forgive us. At one level, faith is about admitting that we need this forgiveness, and accepting God's offer.

Or think of presenting someone with a gift. Many of us put a lot of thought into gifts, believing they reflect our love or affection for the person we want to receive them. A friend of mine, knowing that I liked the writings of C. S. Lewis, once gave me a first edition of *Surprised by Joy*, Lewis's autobiography. I was very touched. Why? Because it showed that he knew me, and wanted me to have something that I would really like. Accepting a gift is both about receiving a benefit and acknowledging the generosity and thoughtfulness of the giver. Martin Luther had no doubt of how precious the gift of salvation was: Jesus has obtained this, 'not with silver nor gold, but with his own precious blood', and he offers it to us, freely and lovingly.

In Jesus, God makes it possible for us to receive and possess forgiveness, reconciliation and the hope of eternal life – things that we could never achieve by ourselves, or ever afford to buy. We might think of faith as an empty, open hand, stretching out towards a gracious and giving

God. Unless we accept and receive the gift that is offered, it will not benefit us.

Or we can consider linking up with Christ in medical terms. Remember my earlier analogy of a course of penicillin? Picture a bottle of penicillin tablets on a table in front of you, and then consider the possible attitudes you might have to it. You might read the label and think to yourself, 'This could change the life of someone suffering from blood poisoning.' But you're perfectly healthy, so that's completely by the way. It's not relevant to you.

Now imagine that you have developed blood poisoning. Suddenly, the penicillin becomes rather more interesting. It could save your life. But it's not going to help you if it stays in the bottle – you need to take it! Drugs only heal when they get into our bloodstream.

There's a nice parallel here with faith. Theologians have often used medical models and analogies to express the transformative impact of the Christian gospel on individuals. Augustine of Hippo (358–430), for example, argued that God's grace healed spiritual blindness and restored people to spiritual health. The Church, he suggested, could be thought of as a hospital – a place in which wounded and broken people might receive medication and care.

Faith is about allowing ourselves to be healed and transformed. Jesus does not heal us by external example but by internal transformation. His power to save does not lie in telling us what God is like but in becoming an incarnate personal presence within our lives. The bread of life must be eaten; the water which springs up to eternal life must be drunk; the healing salve of the gospel must be applied. The old African-American spiritual got this exactly right:

> There is a balm in Gilead
> To make the wounded whole;
> There is a balm in Gilead
> To heal the sin-sick soul.

Our souls will be healed if we take the balm, apply it and allow it to do its God-given and God-empowered work.

Finally, we can think of faith in terms of connecting up with a greater story. We might think of C. S. Lewis's insight that faith involves our own stories becoming part of a bigger story, and being transformed as a result. We are embraced by God, and become part of the story of God. We are now part of something that gives meaning to our lives, and helps us work out what we are meant to be doing.

Now there is more that needs to be said about all of these approaches. For example, I have spoken loosely about 'connecting up' with Jesus of Nazareth. Yet the Christian doctrine of grace makes it clear that we don't do this on our own. God helps us. Grace is the power Jesus of Nazareth gives us to make us like him. Some well-known images from John's Gospel illustrate this point.

The 'I am' sayings and our relationship with Jesus of Nazareth

Every now and then, I come across something that makes me sit up and think. Many years ago now, I read these words in a book by the sixteenth-century writer Philipp Melanchthon (1497–1560): 'To know Christ is to know his benefits'. It was punchy and to the point. We cannot properly 'know' Jesus of Nazareth unless we're also aware of the transformative impact he has on our lives. But what kind of difference does he make? And how does this come into effect?

We find some helpful pointers in the famous 'I am' sayings, one of the most distinctive features of John's Gospel. There are seven such sayings, each with the same structure – for example, 'I am the light of the world' (8.12) and 'I am the true vine' (15.1). The statements echo the 'I AM' language used by God in the Old Testament (Exodus 3.14), and use images that are deeply rooted in the history of Israel to clarify both the significance of Jesus himself, and his relationship to believers. Let's look at three of these 'I am' statements, and see how they help us think about connecting with Jesus.

First, let us reflect on the words 'I am the bread of life' (John 6.35). Jesus speaks these words in the context of feeding a crowd with fish and bread. Human beings have deep physical needs – such as hunger. But they also have spiritual needs, and the verses following this saying use the images of eating and drinking as ways of thinking about faith. 'Those who eat my flesh and drink my blood have eternal life, and I will raise them up on the last day' (John 6.54). When I eat a piece of bread or drink a glass of water, its contents become part of me. They are assimilated into my body. Similarly, faith is about making Jesus of Nazareth part of me. There's an obvious connection with the bread and wine of the Lord's Supper (which we shall consider in more detail in the final volume of this series).

Our second 'I am' saying speaks of Jesus in terms that echo Psalm 23. 'I am the good shepherd' (John 10.11). This beautiful image contrasts Jesus's care for his flock with that of 'hirelings', who have no concern for it. 'The good shepherd lays down his life for the sheep', whereas the hirelings run away the moment danger threatens. We get a powerful sense of Jesus' love for and commitment to his people, and a hint that, without him, we are likely to get lost. The first generations of Christians saw Jesus the Good Shepherd as a source of strength and consolation in the face of hostility and persecution within the Roman Empire. Faith was about making a principled decision to entrust themselves to one they knew loved them, and had given his life for them. They had heard his voice call them by name, and there was no other they would follow.

The third saying we shall consider is this: 'I am the true vine' (John 15.1). The Old Testament often spoke of Israel as God's vine, and this verse emphasizes the continuity between the Old and New Testaments, while highlighting Jesus' role as the culmination of the Law and the Prophets. It invites us to think of believers as branches whose wellbeing and growth depend on being connected to the stock of the vine. If they become detached, they will cease to receive the nourishment they need for existence and will die. 'I am the vine, you are the branches. Those who abide in me and I in them bear much fruit, because apart from me you can do nothing' (John 15.5). The image of 'abiding' has become deeply seared into the Christian imagination. Faith is about remaining securely attached to Jesus, relying on his strength and ability to sustain us.

For some Christian spiritual writers, such as Thomas à Kempis, attachment to Jesus demands detachment from the world. For most, however, it means that we are called to engage with the world, without sharing all its ideas and values. Christians are to be light and salt to the world, to act as 'ambassadors' for Jesus of Nazareth (2 Corinthians 5.20). The notion of being 'in the world but not of the world' expresses this critical attitude well, and we shall consider it more fully in our reflections on the Christian life in the final volume of this series.

Jesus and the shape of the Christian life

A colleague of mine lectures in ethics. One day, I asked him to tell me in a few words what ethics was all about. I needed a short sentence to add to a sermon I was preparing, and wanted to make sure that I said something sensible. 'That's easy,' he said. 'You can sum ethics up in just two little words: *be good!*' I was not entirely convinced by this. 'What do you mean by "good"?' I asked him. He frowned. 'That's when it starts getting complicated,' he replied. Why? Because 'good' is such a general and vague term. Just about everyone wants to do what's right. The problem is that they can't agree on what the word 'good' means.

Christianity has always held that God is the supreme good, and that our true destiny lies in trying to do what God wants. 'Be imitators of God, as beloved children, and live in love, as Christ loved us and gave himself up for us' (Ephesians 5.1–2). Some atheists argue that this is about arbitrary submission to some kind of heavenly despot. It's not. It's like being in love with someone who is very fond of daffodils. When you visit, you give that person daffodils. Why? Because you care for the person, and you know that this will please him or her. At the heart of any good relationship is a desire to please those we love. Love for another is both a motivation and guide for how we behave.

So how do we know what God is like, and what God wants? In the end, the best Christian answer to this question is to say that Jesus of Nazareth shows us both what God is like, and what God wants from us. Jesus is not simply the basis of the redeemed life; he is also the model for that life. The heartbeat of the Christian life is a desire to be like Jesus of Nazareth. Knowing Jesus as our Lord motivates and animates

111

us, making us want to serve him. As Oswald Sanders once put it, 'God does not have to come and tell me what I must do for Him, He brings me into a relationship with Himself wherein I hear His call and understand what He wants me to do, and I do it out of sheer love to Him.'

Christian ethics is thus about being 'Christ-like'. It's about asking what Jesus of Nazareth might do in the situations in which we find ourselves. This basic idea is expressed in the famous 'bidding prayer', which opens the service of Nine Lessons and Carols at King's College, Cambridge every year by recalling the compassion of Jesus of Nazareth for the poor and dispossessed. 'And because this of all things would rejoice his heart, let us at this time remember in his name the poor and the helpless, the cold, the hungry and the oppressed.'

Discipleship is about becoming more like Jesus of Nazareth, and 'crucifying' the Old Adam. Paul puts it like this: 'I have been crucified with Christ; and it is no longer I who live, but it is Christ who lives in me. And the life I now live in the flesh I live by faith in the Son of God, who loved me and gave himself for me' (Galatians 2.19–20). Yet this new obedience and new way of life is not something that we can do by ourselves. The God who inspires us to want to do good also helps us to become good. We shall reflect on this in more depth when we consider some themes concerning the Christian life in the next volume in this series, particularly the place of the Holy Spirit in the life of faith.

Many find C. S. Lewis helpful at this point. In his Chronicles of Narnia, Lewis uses the figure of the noble lion Aslan to help his readers reflect on how Jesus of Nazareth inspires us to want to do good, and informs us about what that good might be.[3] Gilbert Meilaender, one of America's leading moral philosophers, once pointed out how the seven Chronicles of Narnia are more than 'good stories'. They help us to 'build character' by providing us with examples from which we can learn, rather like an apprentice working with a master.[4] Aslan is that master, and Lewis intended us to see him as a 'Christ-figure'.

Lewis portrays Aslan as inspirational, enabling people to see and do things that otherwise would lie beyond their ability or inclination. A rich theology of divine grace nestles within the stories of Aslan's encounters with people (such as Digory) and other inhabitants of Narnia (such as Puzzle, the donkey). Lewis here develops the rich and important idea that it is by contemplating Christ that we are enabled to identify and confront our sin, and resolve to try and become better people. Any attempt to be 'good' involves both breaking the power of sin and embracing the power of God. And both are to be found in Jesus of Nazareth.

Yet there is another respect in which Jesus of Nazareth shapes the Christian life – coping with suffering. In the history of the world, four main answers have been given to the question of suffering. Some hold that suffering is real, and is not going to go away. However, we can take comfort from the fact that life does not go on for ever. In the end, we will die, and once we are dead, suffering will end and we will finally have peace and relief from pain.

Others argue that suffering is an illusion. It is something imagined, not real. If we concentrate hard enough, the illusion will vanish. A third opinion recognizes that suffering is real, but argues that intelligent people ought to be able to rise above this.

The Christian has the fourth answer: God suffered in Christ. God knows what it is like to suffer. The letter to the Hebrews talks about Jesus being our 'sympathetic high priest' (Hebrews 4.15) – someone who suffers along with us. This is indeed a world of suffering; yet, because of who Jesus was and what he did, it can now lead to glory. We suffer in hope, having embraced our redeemer through faith.

Focusing on the suffering of Jesus of Nazareth on the cross helps us see suffering in a new way. As Paul points out, 'the sufferings of this present time are not worth comparing with the glory about to be revealed to us' (Romans 8.18). If we suffer with Jesus, we shall one day be glorified with him. Instead of being faced with a hopeless end, we can embrace an endless hope.

Moving on

In this volume, we have looked at some aspects of the creeds' statements about the identity and significance of Jesus of Nazareth. There is much more that needs to be said. We have only had space enough to look all too briefly at some of the great themes of the creeds, as they focus on the central figure of the Christian faith. In the next volume in this series, *Spirit of the Living God*, we shall move on to consider the 'Spirit of Grace'. What do the creeds and the Christian faith have to say about the Holy Spirit, human nature and the Church?

Notes

Introduction

1 Pope Francis, *Evangelii Gaudium* ('The Joy of the Gospel'), 36. For the full text, see <http://www.vatican.va/holy_father/francesco/apost_exhortations/documents/papa-francesco_esortazione-ap_20131124_evangelii-gaudium_en.html>

2 Pope Francis, *Evangelii Gaudium*, 1.

1 Jesus of Nazareth: the turning point

1 C. S. Lewis, *The Lion, the Witch and the Wardrobe*. London: HarperCollins, 2002, 65.

2 For the background, see Martin Hengel, *The Atonement: The Origins of the Doctrine in the New Testament*. London: SCM Press, 1981.

3 J. R. R. Tolkien, *The Monsters and the Critics and Other Essays*. London: HarperCollins, 1997, 153.

4 G. K. Chesterton, *Orthodoxy*. London: Bodley Head, 1909, 258.

2 Jesus of Nazareth: assembling the big picture

1 Pope Francis, *Evangelii Gaudium* ('The Joy of the Gospel'), 12. For the full text, see <http://www.vatican.va/holy_father/francesco/apost_exhortations/documents/papa-francesco_esortazione-ap_20131124_evangelii-gaudium_en.html>

3 Incarnation: the Word became flesh

1 Abraham Pais, *J. Robert Oppenheimer: A Life*. Oxford: Oxford University Press, 2006, 90.

2 Epiphany, traditionally observed on 6 January, marks the visit of the Magi or 'wise men' to visit Jesus (Matthew 2.1–12). The unusual word 'epiphany' is derived from a Greek word which means 'to show forth' or 'to manifest'.

3 Dorothy L. Sayers, *Creed or Chaos?* London: Methuen, 1947, 24.

4 For a good introduction to these early debates, see Alister E. McGrath, *Christian Theology: An Introduction.* 5th edn. Oxford: Wiley-Blackwell, 2011, 265–94.

5 For an introduction to the idea of heresy, see Alister E. McGrath, *Heresy: A History of Defending the Truth.* London: SPCK, 2010.

6 For an excellent study, see Rowan Williams, *Arius: Heresy and Tradition.* Grand Rapids, MI: Eerdmans, 2002.

7 Larry W. Hurtado, *Lord Jesus Christ: Devotion to Jesus in Earliest Christianity.* Grand Rapids, MI: Eerdmans, 2003; Richard Bauckham, *Jesus and the God of Israel.* Grand Rapids, MI: Eerdmans, 2008.

8 2 Clement 1.1. This letter probably dates from the early second century, although there is some uncertainty about its date.

9 As recalled by one of his students, Thomas F. Torrance (1913–2007): see Thomas F. Torrance, 'Hugh Ross MacKintosh: Theologian of the Cross'. *Scottish Bulletin of Evangelical Theology* 5 (1987), 160–73; quote at 163.

10 John Calvin, *Institutes of the Christian Religion*, II.13.4.

11 Jürgen Moltmann, *Jesus Christ for Today's World.* Minneapolis, MN: Fortress Press, 71.

12 Athanasius, *On the Incarnation of the Word of God*, 8.

13 Letter to Arthur Greeves, 18 October, 1931; *The Collected Letters of C. S. Lewis.* 3 vols. San Francisco: HarperOne, 2004–6, vol. 1, 976.

14 C. S. Lewis, 'The Grand Miracle', in *C. S. Lewis: Essay Collection.* London: Collins, 2000, 3–9.

4 Atonement: putting things right

1 For a full discussion, see Alister E. McGrath, *Christian Theology: An Introduction.* 5th edn. Oxford: Wiley-Blackwell, 2011, 315–47.

2 A similar line of thought lies behind the poet John Donne's lines: 'We think that Paradise and Calvary, Christ's cross and Adam's tree, stood in one place.'

3 *Catechism of the Catholic Church*, §608.

4 C. S. Lewis, 'On Forgiveness', in *C. S. Lewis: Essay Collection*. London: Collins, 2000, 184–6.

5 Jesus of Nazareth and the life of faith

1 *The Works of Richard Hooker*. 8 vols. London: Clarke, 1821, vol. 3, 369. The image, which is based on Romans 13.14 ('put on Christ' or 'clothe yourselves with Christ'), is also found in earlier writers.

2 See Anne E. Matter, 'Mystical Marriage', in *Women and Faith: Catholic Religious Life in Italy from Late Antiquity to the Present*, ed. Lucetta Scaraffia and Gabriella Zarri. Cambridge, MA: Harvard University Press, 1999, 30–41.

3 See Alister McGrath, *Deep Magic, Dragons and Talking Mice: How Reading C. S. Lewis Can Change Your Life*. London: Hodder & Stoughton, 2014, 35–66.

4 Gilbert Meilaender, *The Taste for the Other: The Social and Ethical Thought of C. S. Lewis*. Grand Rapids, MI: Eerdmans, 1978, 212–13.